Studies in Tagore

Critical Essays

Studies in Tagore

Critical Essays

SANTOSH CHAKRABARTI

ATLANTIC
PUBLISHERS & DISTRIBUTORS

Published by
ATLANTIC PUBLISHERS AND DISTRIBUTORS
B-2, Vishal Enclave, Opp. Rajouri Garden, New Delhi-27
Phones : 25413460, 25429987, 25466842

Sales Office
7/22, Ansari Road, Darya Ganj, New Delhi-110 002
Phones : 23273880, 23275880, 23280451
Fax : 91-11-23285873
web : www.atlanticbooks.com
e-mail : info@atlanticbooks.com

ISBN 81-269-0340-6

Printed in India at
Nice Printing Press, Delhi

DEDICATED TO

My Wife

Sumitra

PREFACE

Tagore, with his polyvalent personality, is a perennial source of interest to people at home and abroad. Apart from their abiding literary value, his writings are significant because they enshrine his views on the myriad aspects of life, which are in no way dated. His novels and short stories are riveted to the socio-familial problems of the times in which he lived. But their greatest merit lies in their transcendence of the immediate time and place and their relevance to the present-day Indian society. More significantly, his study of the women, especially from the psychological angle, reveals an ever-sensitive mind, keen perception and clarity of vision which make his writings so interesting and exceptional.

This Volume comprises a bunch of critical essays mainly on his novels and short stories focusing on his views on communalism, gender question, man-woman relationship and contentious issues of contemporary Bengal.

I take this opportunity to express my gratitude to Mr. Satinath Roy, retired Deputy Director of Information, Government of West Bengal, whose inspiration produced some of these papers and to Dr. Mohit K. Ray, Professor of English, Burdwan University (West Bengal) for giving me valuable advice regarding publication of the book.

I am thankful to Dr. K.R. Gupta, Chairman, M/s Atlantic Publishers and Distributors, for publishing the book.

SANTOSH CHAKRABARTI

CONTENTS

1

Patriarchy, Feminist Thought and Tagore's Heroines

The importance of novels and short stories in the *oeuvre* of Tagore is great, because here the scope for presentation of the problems of life is far greater and as a matter of fact the problems arising out of the complexities of man-woman relationship and their possible solutions have also been portrayed in greater detail. In the present paper an attempt has been made to focus on Tagore's feminist outlook and his outlook on women's progress in the social set-up of his own times in the context of the centuries-old patriarchal concept and practice in the country through a discussion of the lives and problems of a few select women characters of his novels and short stories.

A patriarchal society is not liberal in conceding its women segment any right and so women's dignity is a glorious exception in a conservative patriarchal set-up. Any attempt at women's progress and/or giving equal rights to women shakes the society to its foundation. Tagore's epoch-making short story *Streer Patra* (The Wife's Letter) invited protest letters from the conservative segment of the public when the story was published in *Sabujpatra,* Sravan issue, 1321 B.S. Bipin Chandra Pal's *Mrinaler Patra* and Lalit Chandra Bandyopadhyay's *Swamir Patra* published in the monthly journal *Narayan* were not only scathingly critical of the writer of *Streer Patra* but predicted chaos and doom in the family and social life. This progressive and feminist outlook of Tagore espousing women's emancipation was not only the result of his personal thinking, it imbibed also the progressivist thinking of the West. 'It cannot be said that in our society the women had no value; as daughter, wife and mother the woman claimed a romantic outlook and hence love and respect, but outside the family relations the woman had no value as woman; not only in our country, but in any country of the world. The value of the woman is a comparatively recent discovery, the result of socio-economic evolution. This discovery was first made in Europe and other Western countries at the beginning of the 19th century, but this discovery made its impact in the third and fourth decades of that century and its full-fledged expression was observed after the first World War. *Streer Patra* was the first indication of the impact of that wave on our calm unruffled shores' (*Rabindra-sahityer Bhumika,* Niharranjan Ray, 1369 B.S., 375).

Rabindranath's mind was exercised over the question of women's emancipation since quite a few years before this revolutionary discourse on Mrinal's individualism and emancipation in *Streer Patra.* Ever since the beginning of the 20th century in Bengal, especially in the middle-class society of urban Bengal, individualism became a strong force in life. In an enlightening discourse on the evolutionary process of this society Dr. Niharranjan Ray says that in the narrow space of conjugality, that is, at the micro level of husband-wife relationship as against the macro level of larger family life 'modern husband and wife wish for the independent existence of this close personal relationship. In the mother-in-law-dominated family the identity of the woman does not lie in attaining the position of the daughter-in-law, her other—more important—identity lies in the realization of a close independent family-exclusive conjugal relationship. This sense of individuality expresses itself in a desire for an independent existence for the woman as woman quite distinct from her husband in the most recent Bengali society.... The inevitable result of this sense of individuality is the sense of sexual freedom of the woman' (*ibid.,* 404). The personality and sexual independence of Binodini in Tagore's *Chokher Bali* (The Eyesore) are the inevitable results of this twentieth-century concept of individualism.

In Indian society the presence of child widows became inevitable in middle-class homes because of the custom of unequal marriage between tender-aged girls and old men.

Then, on the one hand, their harsh life-style brought them untold misery and on the other, their natural youthful growth and repressed sexual urges helped develop a socially unacceptable illicit sex-relationship with the younger male members of the family. The sex feelings that arise in the mind of Binodini very naturally make her jealous of the Mahendra-Asha conjugality. Again, the jealousy that has been created in her seeing the excess of affection in Bihari for Asha is another expression of her repressed sexual feelings (it must be remembered that Binodini is a child-widow). Tagore writes: 'Bihari could not see Binodini's face in the dark, envy flashed on her face. Today seeing Bihari she understood that his heart was tormented with pity for Asha. Binodini herself was none! She was born only to shield Asha, only to remove all the thorns from her path and only to help in the full realization of Asha's happiness! Srijukta Mahendra Babu would marry Asha, and so under the machinations of fate Binodini would have to live with wild monkeys at Barasat, Srijukta Bihari Babu cannot bear innocent Asha shedding tears. So Binodini would always have to stand ready with the end of her sari. Once Binodini wants to show this Mahendra and this Bihari who is Asha and who is Binodini by lowering them to the dust along with the shadow at her back! She was to show what a great difference exists between them! Because of adverse fate having failed to unobtrusively ensconce her talent in the mind of a man, Binodini assumed the form of destruction by wielding the fiery *saktishel*' (*Rabindra Upanyas-samgraha,* Visva-Bharati, 1990, 229, translated). According to Freud moral development coincides with the development of the super-ego. The most significant moment in the development of the super-ego in boys, in the resolution of the Oedipus complex, arises from the fear of castration. In the case of little girls the question of this fear does not arise and therefore in them the resolution of the Oedipus complex is not as complete as in boys with the result that their centre of morality remains underdeveloped. In other words, in Freud's view the sense of morality is less developed in girls than in boys. Though these views of Freud have now come to be contested by recent researchers, Binodini's desire for establishing a covert illicit relationship with Mahendra seems to have a

Freudian perspective. But in real terms what is discernible in this desire is more of game-playing than sincerity. True, she has expressed the hunger of her heart to Mahendra in letters written on behalf of Asha, but she has never capitulated herself to the sex advances of Mahendra. The object of her love is Bihari, not Mahendra; this at least is proved by her submission to Bihari after Mahendra proposes to elope with her: "'Lord of my life, I know that you are not mine eternally, but kindly love me for a moment today. Then I will retire to our forests, without demanding anything from anybody. Give me something which I can remember till death.' Saying this Binodini advanced her lips towards Bihari closing her eyes" (*ibid.*, 277, translated). Mahendra's love advances have been rejected the umpteen times, and when at last she agrees to leave home with Mahendra, it is only to go in search of the fugitive Bihari. Only once does Binodini come close to submitting herself to Mahendra's sexuality when during Asha's sojourn to Benares, she is drawn to him in the name of nursing him in his illness: 'Sitting near his head when she was mildly massaging his forehead, Binodini's head was slowly being bent under the heavy weight of her confounded youth; at last the tips of her locks touched Mahendra's forehead. By the shaken slight touch of the wind-wafted hair locks his whole body began to tremble repeatedly, suddenly his breath seemed to get stuck near his breast and found no outlet' (*ibid.*, 254, translated). It is conjecturable whether this incident shows her attraction for Mahendra, or whether it shows the naturally jealous woman's attempt at creating fissures in the Mahendra-Asha relationship.

Rabindranath has portrayed two contradictory personas of Binodini. In fact she embodies the two opposite personas of a woman—she is the source of familial and societal good/well-being and she is destructive. To Bihari her part-overt identity is that she is 'a beautiful riddle' and again, like 'the planet Saturn' she takes on the embodiment of destruction by destroying 'the love of a friend, conjugal love, and the peace and sanctity of the home' (*ibid.*, 279, translated). For creating fissures in the Mahendra-Asha conjugal relationship her identity to Rajlakshmi is that of an 'enchantress' (*ibid.*, 271). Yet it was this enchantress whom once Rajlakshmi used for her own end—"Binodini restrained herself from saying something but said, 'It's true, Auntie, nobody knows anybody. Does anybody know his/her own mind? Did you never want to wean away the mind of your son through this enchantress out of jealousy for your daughter-in-law? Try to remember.'" (*Ibid.*, 272, translated.) The history of Mahendra-Rajlakshmi relationship has an Oedipal perspective. Binodini is Asha's double to Rajlakshmi out of jealousy for her daughter-in-law. But when the same Binodini has decentralised Mahendra, then Rajlakshmi with her motherly authority has sought to restrict her manoeuvrability and limit her space.

However Rabindranath has not lowered the Mahendra-Binodini relationship to the level of illicit sexuality and on the other hand kept the Bihari-Binodini relationship at the idealised Platonic level. Just as Mahendra has reverted to the secure domestic fold of Asha's love being finally rejected by Binodini at the Allahabad garden-house, so Binodini too has accepted Platonic love as the ideal of her life after rejecting Bihari's offer of marriage with due reverence and greedlessness:

> *Binodini.* Fie, Fie, I'm ashamed to think of this. I am a widow, tainted; shall I shame you before the whole society? I can never allow it to happen. Fie, fie, don't utter such things (*ibid.*, 322, translated).

By not conceding widow remarriage while foregrounding Binodini's individuality and sexual independence Rabindranath has practically accepted the age-old tradition.

Rabindranath has made extensive experiments on women's emancipation and sexual freedom in a number of novels and short stories in order to express his views on the gender question. But the trend of his feminist ideas, like Hardy's, is not uniform. In *Chokher Bali* his feminism beats retreat ultimately, but in the short story entitled *Nashtanir* (The Broken Home) which was composed in the same time span when *Chokher Bali* was written, he is very progressive in portraying the triangular love of Bhupati, Charu and Amal. Again *Streer Patra* (The Wife's Letter, published in 1321 B.S.) is a bold step on the question of women's emancipation. In *Chaturanga* (Four Aspects), published in 1322 B.S., he sought to strike a hard blow on the citadel of conservatism by bringing about widow remarriage. He is once again a bit retrogressive in *Ghare-Baire* (The Home and the World, 1323 B.S.) and *Yogayog* (Communication, 1334 B.S.). In *Yogayog* especially he seems to sound a bit discordant. Again in the short story *Laboratory* written towards the end of his life his feminist attitude seems to take the most meaningful shape. Thomas Hardy too evinces a similarly uneven attitude on the gender question. The feminist stance noticed in *The Return of the Native* (1878) takes an about-turn in *The Mayor of Casterbridge* in which Hardy seems to be blatantly patriarchal. Even in the heroine of *Far From the Madding Crowd* (1874) there is an expression of self-beguiling and spontaneous sexual fervour which has given her personality an effulgent glow. And Sue Bridehead, the heroine of *Jude the Obscure* is a representative of the class of the 'New Woman' that heralds the New Age. It is possible to discern the characteristics of the 'New Woman' in the heroine of *Laboratory,* Sohini.

Damini of *Chaturanga* is a rebel. A young widow, Damini is 'as it were lightning within the fold of Sravan clouds. Externally dollops of youth make up her body; internally moving fire is burning with flashes.... That woman is a stranger to death, she drinks deep in the fount of life. Like the flower bower of spring she always fills herself with grace, fragrance and gaiety; she does not want to throw away anything, she does not like to entertain a *sanyasi* in her home; she has pledged not to pay any rent to the north wind' (*ibid.*, 814).

She is a rebel since the death of her husband; in the thin thread of her conjugal life there was no love, only her life had become subjected to untold misery by the 'tyranny of devotion.' So the unsatiated desire of her body and mind has taken the form of rebellion after the death of her husband. In Lilanandaswami's *ashram* the women devotees 'would be struck dumb by seeing Damini's activities. On the one hand her dress was not like a widow's, on the other she cared a fig for the sage sermon of the guru. Moreover there was no sign in her of the enlightened state of the mind and body through restraint and purity which would spontaneously envelop anybody if he lived close to such a great enlightened personality' (*ibid.*, 816).

But a short while after the arrival of Sachish in the *ashram* she undergoes a change which is nothing but the expression of her passion of love. 'The hard shell of her rebellion burnt silently and the flower of her self-surrender raised its bedewed face upwards' (*ibid.*, 816). But Sachish has not given any value to this attitude of surrender of Damini, for within a short space of time she gets Sachish's kick and refusal in his semi-awakened and semi-drowsy state. This single incident is the watershed in her life and changes the habitual and so-far-accustomed course of her life. On the one hand there is the surrender of Damini—'After that something got round my leg.... It seemed as if it was a serpent-like creature, which I didn't know. What was its head like, what sort of a body it had, what sort of a tail I knew nothing—I couldn't think out what was the process of its swallowing. It was so terrible because it was so soft, that lump of hunger!' (*Ibid.*, 818). On the other hand there is Sachish's hard, forceful refusal—'I began to push it away with both my legs. It seemed it had placed its mouth on my feet—it was breathing fast—I didn't know what sort of a face it was. I kicked at it throwing my legs repeatedly' (*ibid.*, 818). But this incident has a great impact on the evolution of her life-mode. In the next stage her overt partiality for and favour to Sribilas are nothing but an expression of her indirect protest to Sachish's stolid indifference to her. Rabindranath has sought to explore the mystery of the innermost depths of her mind while revealing the true character of this independent-minded woman. Just as it is true that Damini's interest now lies in arousing jealousy in Sachish, it is equally true that in Sachish's mind has arisen a new restlessness: 'Sachish has undergone a strange metamorphosis.... Externally Sachish is a regular in the routine activities of meditation and worship, but a close look reveals how he has lost his moorings internally' (*ibid.*, 824, translated). Almost according to the rule of woman-excluding religious pursuits of the male devotees, sometimes Sachish asks her to keep away from the hallowed precincts of the *ashram*, and sometimes he asks her to mingle with the group, keeping a low profile. That is, he wants to dispel his newly-awakened weakness for Damini through a neutral and unspecific relationship. In this way Rabindranath has sketched the history of Sachish-Damini relationship through the skein of attraction and repulsion and has shown how in spite of the kick/rejection from the object of her love, a slight show of kindness could bring about a change in the mind and conduct of the love-hungry woman. Considering Damini as an obstacle to his devotional pursuits and asceticism he has asked her to leave the *ashram* (Damini's journey to Calcutta accompanied by Sribilas is actually undertaken to honour this advice of Sachish), but Damini has elevated her passion for Sachish to the level of reverence-oriented love through a process of mental evolution. A sequel to this evolutionary process is her acceptance of Sachish as her guru: "Damini said, 'Be my guru. I shall not accept anybody else. Teach me such a *mantra* which is far above all these things—so that I can save myself from going astray'" (*ibid.*, 828, translated).

The novel is surely a landmark in feminist thinking. Not only has Tagore made a bold and decisive assault on the age-old conservative thinking by bringing about the marriage between Sribilas and widowed Damini, but he has also accorded due importance to the individuality of a woman by prioritising Sachish as the object of true love over Sribilas in the heart of Damini. That Damini rises above Binodini is proved by the fact that the question of society and public calumny does not deter her from the path of marriage. The proposal of marriage comes from her:

> "I (Sribilas) said, 'What do you call the real thing?'
> 'Say, what will befall you if you marry me.'"
>
> (*Ibid.*, 838, translated)

Though conscious of her individual freedom, Damini cannot deny the truth of her love for Sachish. Sachish's cruel rejection—symbolised by the kick which has pushed her slowly towards death—is the only positive factor in her life. It is a kind of masochism, the height of love nurtured by pain. Her clean confession to Sribilas before her death—'This pain is my secret treasure, my touchstone. This is the dowry which helped me to come to you, or am I fit for you?' (*ibid.*, 840)—has added a new dimension to her femininity.

In *Ghare-Baire* (The Home and the World) Tagore is again a traditionalist. Here in this novel Bimala wants to live the life of a traditional Hindu woman according to the age-old Indian custom. Since her mother is the exemplar of traditional Hindu womanhood to her, she expresses a desire at the very outset of the novel to mould herself on her mother's ideal—'Mother, I remember today the vermilion mark on the parting of your hair, that red-bordered sari, those two eyes of yours—calm, mellow, deep. I have seen them as the crimson ray of the sun at dawn in my mind's sky, that started his journey on my day of days with the golden provision. I am not handsome, but I prayed to God that I might be given the glory of a chaste woman like my mother' (*ibid.*, 847, translated). In her in-laws' house Bimla has tried to mould herself as an ideal Hindu woman. Though she has to live within the inner apartment of the house she has no sense of want in her life. At the beginning of the novel her psycho-physical needs do not assume any unmanageable proportion. She feels no urge for mixing with the outside world, on the other hand, she is averse to it. Under the impression that the husband is the living god in this mortal life for a woman, she has formed the habit of taking the dust off her husband's feet while leaving bed in the morning—'I remember, getting out of bed when I surreptitiously took the dust off my husband's feet, the vermilion mark at the parting of my hair seemed to dazzle like the morning star' (*ibid.*, 848, translated). From such an ideal Indian woman Nikhilesh's (in the Macmillan English translation 'Nikhilesh' has been made 'Nikhil') expectations are of a strange, different sort, unconventional, to say the least. By taking her out into the 'outside' world and allowing her sufficient independence he wants to prove his own superiority and claim greater love from her:

> My husband had a fond desire to take me out. One day I said to him, 'What need I to go out?'
>
> He said, 'The outside may need you....'
>
> 'I want that you get me through the outside, and I get you in the same manner. It is there that our mutual dealings have not yet been done....'
>
> 'Here your eyes, ears, face have been kept covered with my help—You do not know whom you want, nor whom you have got' (*ibid.*, 852, translated).

In this way the kind of freedom that her liberal-humanist husband has sought to give is the more cultured and enlightened version of women's independence. He does not accept the argument in favour of confining the wife to the *antahpur* of the house. So his fervent wish is that by tasting freedom she should know herself, know the outside world and her husband. Tagore has in this novel manner made a discourse of male-endowed freedom to women: Bimala is allowed space without struggle.

Though Bimala is not at first agreeable to the idea of 'going out' an opportunity comes when the *Swadeshi* wave sweeps away the thoughts and fears of everybody before anybody can understand anything. But what has happened to Bimala's life in the name of her going out is not only pernicious to her life but has a pernicious effect in her conjugal life. The impressive robes and oratory of Nikhilesh's friend Sandip have created in her an infatuation which has swept away her ideals of Indian womanhood and belied the ever-felt truth about conjugal happiness. Thrown off the orbit of placid domesticity under the impact of *Swadeshi* ideals Bimala feels, 'So long I had been a small river of the village—then I had one rhythm, one language. But suddenly without giving any notice came the deluge of the sea—my breast heaved, my shores were overflooded; the symphony of my current rang to the drum-beat of the sea; I could not decipher the meaning of that sound within my blood-stream. Where did the old self of mine go? From where did the wave of beauty come suddenly swelling in me? The unsatiated pair of Sandip Babu's eyes as if burned towards my beauty with the glow of the lamp of worship' (*ibid.*, 870, translated). Bimala has been slowly weaned away from Nikhilesh by the twin forces of Sandip's magnetic power and her own false sense of self-glory ('Gradually I had a conviction that Sandip Babu was at the root of every work that was being done in the whole country, and the guiding force of it all was the simple, innocuous intelligence of an insignificant woman. My mind was filled with the glory of a vast responsibility.'—*Ibid.*, 871, translated). Sandip's philosophy ('The teaching of the whole world is that whatever I can snatch away is mine proper' (*ibid.*, 867, translated), his discussion on sex relationship between men and women completely outside the scope of *Swadeshi* matters, addiction to women (his connection with the widowed Kusum and an Anglo-Indian girl for example, and his feeling of pride thereof) and his irresistible attraction to Bimala etc. have as much unmasked him as pushed Bimala to the brink. Bimala develops a dichotomial attitude towards Sandip very soon: she knows that she has a false infatuation for Sandip and yet she cannot get out of it. It is a dichotomy which divides her into two (*ibid.*, 883).

On the one hand Bimala is thrown off the domestic fold under Sandip's magnetic pull, and on the other, her infatuation for the outside has rendered Nikhilesh's home derelict and lifeless. It cannot be contested that this husband-wife rupture is the result of the licence that Nikhilesh allows her at the first instance. On the other hand with a low hedonistic mindset Sandip contemplates enjoying personal pleasure at the cost of Bimala when he asks her to give him fifty thousand rupees in the country's cause. Caught between a sense of duty and the call of the country (a fake call though) Bimala is forced to steal *mohurs* from her husband's (that is, her own) iron safe. But when Sandip rushes forward greedily to take the *mohurs* from her, she pushes him with all her might so much so that he falls to the ground. This theft is the most crucial point in the Bimala-Sandip relationship, for her realisation of guilt forces the reverse journey from the *world* to *home*, from Sandip to Nikhilesh: 'The moment I handed over the money after committing a theft on my husband's coffers, the very music of our relationship was gone' (*ibid.*, 938, translated). The next part of the story features a repentant Bimala's surrender and home-coming. In the words of Nikhilesh, "She began to bow her head down to my feet repeatedly, kneeling after freeing her hands from mine a little forcibly. As soon as I took away my feet she clasped both my feet and with an emotion-filled voice said, 'No, no, no, do not take away your feet. Let me worship you'" (*ibid.*, 964, translated).

In this way Rabindranath has made a discourse of the traditional Indian way of life in the circular structure of Bimala's story and has registered a triumph of patriarchy by highlighting the pitfalls of Bimala's unsolicited empowerment.

Kumu of *Yogayog* (Communication) has waged a life-long battle against the stranglehold of patriarchy ever since her marriage. Though her battle against the loveless sex hunger of her husband becomes successful at the initial stages, ultimately Rabindranath has chalked out a history of her surrender, howsoever reluctant, to patriarchy and the unwritten laws of a male-dominated society.

Madhusudan's attitude to conjugal relationship and his views about bringing a wayward wife under control may seem to be well-intended, but actually they reveal the blatant inhumanity of purpose: 'There is only one way to bind Kumudini with him with a strong knot, and that is the way of forcing motherhood on her' (*ibid.*, 1010, translated). In Madhusudan's thinking the child is not the hyphen-link between husband and wife but a weapon to coerce a recalcitrant wife into submission. As soon as the real identity of Madhusudan is exposed in her first contact with him—especially the way he has forced her to part with the sapphire ring and the way he has hurled insulting words at her absent brother Bipradas, she has come to develop a sort of aversion to her newly-wed husband. This aversion is turned into a sex-aversion and the manner in which she behaves before the consummation of their marriage is a sure enough indicator of the future course of their relationship. Rabindranath has presented this cold relationship in the frame of a pigeon-hawk imagery—'As a she-pigeon behaves seeing the shadow of a hawk from the sky, Kumu's heart seemed to shiver in the same manner. Her cold palm was sweating and her face turned colourless' (*ibid.*, 1005, translated). This is followed by a swoon which is most uncongenial for the first night's husband-wife union. When finally Madhusudan succeeds in coaxing her into sexual union with him which results in her unwanted pregnancy and her most reluctant return to her husband's house, it is true she capitulates, but Tagore has brought out the tragedy of it all with the help of another telling imagery: 'In that silent room there is no more any sound; at the crossing of the road the voice of the drunkard is heard no more; only the chained dog, though tired, cries out intermittently' (*ibid.*, 1036). In order to highlight the ugly aspect of Madhusudan's character Rabindranath has introduced the story of his illicit relationship with Shyamasundari.

At the end of the novel when Madhusudan takes Kumu to his Mirzapur palace with great pomp and eclat, it signals, once again, the triumph of patriarchy. But this picture of triumph seems to be a staunchly sarcastic commentary of Rabindranath on patriarchy itself.

However even if in the literal sense it means the retreat of progressivist forces, Rabindranath has created in the twilight years of his life the true modern woman—in fact the Indian version of the New Woman—in Sohini in the short story, *Laboratory,* by uniting contradictory forces. She is independent-minded, believes in women's empowerment and is not averse to sexual plurality by virtue of her sexual freedom and yet can stake her life for saving her husband's laboratory. That is, by uniting idealism and individualism Sohini is Rabindranath's ideal woman.

2

THE CUPID QUESTION—IN THE PERSPECTIVE OF TAGORE'S NOVELS

One of the paradoxes of Tagore's socio-literary perception is that he reverted to the groove of tradition after breaking fresh grounds in fiction on the Cupid question. If in *Chokher Bali* (The Eyesore), serialised in the revamped *Bangadarshan* journal from Baisakh, 1308 B.S. to Kartik 1309 B.S. he treated the Cupid question in the boldest terms, in *Noukadubi* (The Boat Disaster), serialised in the same journal five months later, from Baisakh, 1310 B.S. to Ashadh, 1312 B.S. he retreated to a safe and sound stance of traditionality.

Emotive, extra-marital and unconventional sex problems that convulsed Tagore's mind in the early years of the 14th century (B.S.) evolved in concrete shapes with their myriad ramifications in *Nashtanir* (The Broken Home), first treated as a novel and later included in his collection of short stories. This novelette[1] which was serialised in the *Bharati* journal contemporaneously with *Chokher Bali* from Baisakh, 1308 B.S. to Agrahayan was possibly written after *Chokher Bali*,[2] but its importance as a seminal work on the problem of emotive love relations lies in the fact that it focused attention on the subject from the angle of free-mixing between a married young woman and an unmarried young brother-in-law, finding succour and nourishment from the neglect of a sex-cold husband; while in *Chokher Bali* the problem is seen from the angle of free-mixing between a married young man and a young full-blossomed widow, finding succour and nourishment from lust. By simultaneously serialising a novelette and a full-length novel in two different prestigious journals, Tagore sought to gauge the reaction of the reading public which was then fed on the portrayal of idyllic romance in novels.

A comparative reference to Bankimchandra's treatment of emotive extra-marital sex and the relational tension and problem developing in the family from it as noticed in, say, *Krishnakanter Will* (The Will of Krishnakanta) will show how Rabindranath took depiction of sex relation to a bold overt level. Though Bankimchandra is the first novelist to discuss problems of incontinent sex urge and its inevitable result in terms of tragic frictional domesticity, he carefully avoids description of overt sex relation even circumventing it by means of a camouflaged contrivance.

At the nascent incipient stage of Gobindalal-Rohini illicit relationship when Gobindalal raises the drowned Rohini from the Baruni pond and goes through the process of oral respiration, he is actuated by something more than the simple saviour spirit:

> "Finding no alternative Gobindalal said to him (the gardener), 'Then you slowly raise her hands in this way, while I blow air into her month. Then slowly lower the hands.' The gardener agreed. He raised the hands (of Rohini) slowly—and Gobindalal, placing his red full-blossomed flower-like lips upon the red full-blossomed flower-like lips (of Rohini), blew air into the mouth of Rohini."[3]

Contrast it with the natural overt description of natural love between husband and wife, where Bankimchandra does not baulk at referring to kissing in a natural context between husband and wife.[4]

Rabindranath too refers to kissing as a form of caressing of the wife by the husband and the reference is brief, natural as in this sequence between Mahendra and Asha in *Chokher Bali*: 'Then Mahendra drew her (Asha) close and kissed her.'[5] But in the passionate description of an illicit love sequence (illicit because of society's strong disapproval of any marital/ love relationship with a widow) in the same novel, he is most bold and even canonizes a taboo subject and breaks the barrier of conventionalism and prudery in literature:

> 'Slowly the effulgent glow of those listless eyes dimmed; those thirst-dried bright eyes became moist with tears and softened and gradually overflowed with deep emotion;

> in a moment that tear-mild form fell near the feet of Bihari and pressed both his legs to her breast with utmost strength—then in a trice growing like an illusory plant on the trellis of Bihari's physique brought up to his lips a kiss-bound face which resembled a just-blossomed fragrant flower.'[6]

But most unconventional is the depiction of desperate insolence with which Mahendra vows *in the presence of his mother* to tear off the bonds of domesticity to live with Binodini:

> "Mahendra's distraught eyes were turned for a moment to his mother's face; then turning to Binodini again Mahendra said, 'I am going away leaving everything, tell me, will you go with me?'"[7]

This professedly outrageous avowal of extra-marital passion and denial of domesticity and that too in the presence of a mother is an aberration which goes verily against the grain of established social mores.

Mahendra's unrestrained incontinence has dogged him to dissolute dissipation. It is not that Asha lacks the fund of love, service and appeal which can satisfy Mahendra's hunger for psycho-physical needs. Rabindranath delineates the newly-wedded love in terms of adolescent prurience, designates it 'a flood of craziness.'[8] Asha's only drawback as a developing woman is her innocuous naivety and huge, almost inexplicable faith in her husband. Even after learning about the illicit relationship between her husband and Binodini from a letter which fortuitously falls into her hand[9] on her return from Benares, she does not develop any ruinous contempt for Mahendra. On the other hand, she silently suffers indignity when her mother-in-law reproaches her for failing to hold her son within the bonds of domesticity.[10] She is a 'doll'[11] compared to Binodini's identity as an 'exquisitely beautiful enigma.'[12]

In the Indian society of the yesteryear when child widows were an inevitable offshoot of child marriage, those hapless creatures had to pass through a rigorous regimen of fasting, observance of religious rites, vegetarianism and myriad social taboos, forcing deprivation of the body and impoverishment of the soul. But such a cruel deprivation and repression had its inevitable and unpalatable, socially intractable problem of illicit sex-relationship between widows and their close relations. Having grown up through neglect and deprivation as a child widow, Binodini develops a kind of insatiable envy at the happy conjugality of Mahendra and Asha. Her flirtatious motive in respect of Mahendra for whom she pours her heart's passion in letters written to him in the name of Asha[13] is her first response to the need for psycho-physical satisfaction. With an easy and malleable Mahendra as the target the wreck of the domestic bond and peace is not at all a difficult proposition. But her hunger is for love and hence possibly realising the preposterous nature of her position in the Mahendra household, she nurtures a sneaking affection for Bihari, ever since he addresses her as 'goddess,'[14] requesting her to save the innocent Asha from the cruel assaults of circumstances. Such an unstinted praise of Binodini sends her rocking with an unspeakable feeling of ecstasy for she never experienced such a distinctive treatment. In fact it is a watershed in Binodini's love-relation. Mahendra's humiliating allegation against Bihari that he loves Asha and his ingratiating offer to Binodini to go away with her are two important milestones in the gradual development of this love. It is passionate, yet short of abiding fulfilment for she knows the societal constraints against it: 'My life's ultimate, I know you are not mine for ever, but do love me for a moment only. After that I shall disappear into the jungles of ours, and never demand anything from anybody. But give me something which I can remember till death.'[15] But even with her secret store of love for Bihari if she persists with her dalliance with Mahendra and allows him to go to the brink, this is because of Bihari's concern for Asha, which is unbearable to her, and Mahendra's incontinence. She stretches Mahendra to the point of no return because she knows the essential weakness of his character.

However, the story of Mahendra's incontinence and sex-urge has a three-stage development: hypocrisy (initially he is shy of striking an acquaintance with Binodini), insolence (he wants to enjoy both Asha and Binodini in the same household like 'a planet served by two moons',[16] a kind of captive adultery which even Gobindalal in *Krishnakanter Will* does not dare engage) and unbridled lust (he wants to go away with his paramour tearing off all familio-marital connections).

Mahendra is a prisoner of incontinence and there are at least three occasions when he dares go to the brink; first, when after Asha's return from Benares he is propelled by his long-suppressed desire towards Binodini's room, the much awaited *abhisar* (love-journey)—if one is permitted to use that word in a male context—aided by the solitariness of the moon-bathed night,[17] but thwarted in the fulfilment of his desire by the unexpected presence of his mother who is lying on the same mat with Binodini; second, when he goes to Binodini in her Pataldanga shelter where she is ensconced temporarily,[18] but again thwarted by his *amour-propre* and Binodini's stolid non-compliance; and third, when in the solitary garden-house of Bihari at Allahabad he hopes to ravish her,[19] but thwarted because he is only an unwanted interloper into the hallowed precincts of Binodini's love as revealed in her bold and unwavering profession of an almost Platonic love for Mahendra's mush-maligned friend: 'He is within the depths of my heart, for whom I have done this make-up.'[20] The comeuppance of Mahendra is complete.

After a sex-propelled passionate interlude Mahendra returns to the safe haven of Asha's love and domesticity through a catharsis of repentance. It is an odyssey not only for 'a greedy-tongued dirty reptile'[21] (Binodini's acerbic description of Mahendra) from lust to repentance and rediscovered domesticity, but also Tagore's preference for the integument of restraint over incontinence.

The paradox of Rabindranath's responses to the Cupid question in the *oeuvre* of his novels is that his very next novel, *Noukadubi* epitomises a reverse journey, *i.e.*, to abstinence. Mahendra is a reformed descendant of Bankimchandra's Gobindalal and a constricted predecessor of Saratchandra's recklessly lustful Suresh (*Grihadaha*/The Burning of the Home). Yet Mahendra's insolent incontinence is a fictional reality, which even his hope for reconstructing his fractured domesticity after reverting to the love of his long-neglected wife cannot wash. But in *Noukadubi* Ramesh is a picture of abstinence, after a few (nearly three) months of sex-relationship with another man's wife, though unwittingly. But the moment he gets at the truth through a maze of cleverly contrived questions he goes through a difficult process of self-restraint which is unimaginable in Mahendra. So here is a clear reversal which shows that Rabindranath has come a long way from *Chokher Bali* even within a short space of time on the Cupid question. Even the low-key description of a burgeoning conjugal—almost puerile—love between Ramesh and Kamala[22] before the crucial revelation adumbrates Rabindranath's intent.

The continuance of Ramesh's love-affair with Hemnalini and their near-marriage are a recuperative interlude in his long drama of uncertainty, suspense and indecision. The Ramesh-Hemnalini affair is characteristically sedate, unemotional and restrained. Ramesh cannot emote to Hemnalini on his carefully concealed chapter of marriage, and complications arising out of an absurd relationship with a woman who is not his wife but he does not know whose and hence his anxiety to find her real husband. But Rabindranath cannot go to the socially unsanctioned length of an inter-caste marriage between a Brahmo girl and a Hindu youth, just as in *Chokher Bali* he cannot bring about the marriage between a young widow and an unmarried young man. Hence Ramesh has to leave Calcutta with Kamala for a westward diaspora[23] abandoning all hope for marrying Hemnalini.

The uneven tug-of-war between a determined Ramesh caught in the predicament of staving off the 'attachment of conjugality' and an unsuspecting Kamala making an earnest endeavour for elevation to the coveted position of 'the mistress of the household'[24] in their brief life in the steamer leads to greater hesitation on Ramesh's part to divulge the truth about their relationship and so he has to muster all his power to resist the temptation of making the situation easy by relational proximity, *i.e.*, by sharing the same bed which is an anathema in the present context. On the other hand, Kamala knows that the edifice of domesticity that she wants to build in her 'small floating household'[25] is to be exorcised of Ramesh's inscrutable indifference to have meaning, purpose and sustenance. Ramesh's unnatural avoidance of her and her claustrophobic separate bed-chamber thrust her into a queer enigmatic world in which she feels abandoned and cloistered: "Her bed-chamber was lonely, dark—on entering, her heart trembled, she felt absolutely deserted and lonely; that small wooden room spread out its own darkness like the opened jaw of some cruel unknown animal. Where would she go? Where would she lay her small body and say closing her eyes—'This one is my own place?'"[26] But Rabindranath cannot for once see the ideal of womanhood besmirched by illicit relation. So Ramesh's predicament is somewhat eased by the induction of the old Chakraborty uncle as a convenient *deus ex machina*. But what makes things intractable for Ramesh is his long association with a woman who does not belong to him and yet with whom he feels a faint longing to unite. A dialectical tension between the interacting pulls of acceptance and avoidance weakens him, brings him near to a premature dissolution of abstinence:

> "Sitting on a chair on the deck of the steamer, Ramesh started pondering. 'This is an impossible state of affairs to carry on. As days pass, life will be more problematic with a rebellious Kamala. It is very difficult to maintain a distance living so near to her. Now I'll give up. Kamala is my wife—I accepted her as my wife. It is unjust to dither because the marriage was not solemnised by *mantras*. The god of death brought Kamala that day to my side as my wife and himself tied the knot on that lonely riverside—where is another priest like him under the sun!'"[27]

The ambience of ease in the Chakraborty household at Gazipur in general and the benign conviviality of Chakraborty's married daughter Shailaja in particular provide the necessary spur to a quick progression from indecision to resolution on Ramesh's part, but at the climactic point of his giving Kamala the much-awaited domestic anchorage in a separate bungalow at Gazipur, Rabindranath inducts another *deus ex machina* which permanently kills the possibility of union between Ramesh and Kamala: Ramesh's letter[28] written to Hemnalini containing the history of Kamala and her awkward relationship with him. The final union of Kamala with her sacramentally tied husband Nalinaksha is the culmination of her individuation that starts in her brief stay in the steamer specially on the question of going to Gazipur[29] and her observance of the Hindu ethos as soon as she discovers that she is another man's wife. But this union which takes place after a tortuous process of trial, uncertainty and eager expectation has a very important, though secondary, offshoot of throwing Ramesh out in the vast uncharted world of redundancy[30] in an ironical pursuit of abstinence!

The abstinence paradigm thus charted out, Rabindranath never veers away from it in his later novels. Even in *Chaturanga* (Four Aspects) serialised about a decade later in 1321 B.S. in *Sabujpatra* he indulges in portraying the interplay of passion in the widowed Damini, even dares bring about widow remarriage (between Damini and Sribilas)—a clear advance on *Chokher Bali*—but does not make a slide-back letting incontinence dominate over abstinence. Damini's desperate foray into Sachish's cave[31] may be passionate, even sex-oriented, but it brings to the fore the strong character content of Sachish who gives repeated kicks on 'the mass of hunger.'[32] In *Ghare-Baire* (The Home and the World) Sandip's magnetic personality, guts and manliness draw Bimala into his incontinent fold—'I have no false sense of shame because Bimala has grown into an object of my (sex) desire. I can clearly see that she wants me, she is my own'[33]—but she is saved from the brink by her own personality and Sandip's metamorphosis in her contact: 'Everything is ruined if one tries to make cheap out of greed that which is the greatest in the world; once one wants to spread in time what is unlimited in the heart of the moment one places it in the narrow confine of limitedness. We were out to destroy that eternal, just when your thunder was raised, and you saved your worship and this worshipper of yours too.'[34] This sublimated realisation relates to his journey from incontinence to abstinence.

This paper started with a focus on Rabindranath's paradoxical reverse role as a novelist. But there is nothing unusual in this stance of Rabindranath, when one considers that the abstinence paradigm was developed in his *Naibedya* (Offering) days.

NOTES AND REFERENCES

1. Prabhat Kr. Mukhopadhyay, *Rabindrajibani*, Vol. II, 1368 B.S., 70.
2. *Ibid.*, 68.
3. *Krishnakanter Will*, Chapter 16.
4. *Ibid.*, Chs. 10 and 14.
5. *Chokher Bali*, Ch. 22.
6. *Ibid.*, Ch. 37.
7. *Ibid.*, Ch. 34.
8. *Ibid.*, Ch. 15.
9. *Ibid.*, Ch. 33.
10. *Ibid.*, Ch. 42.
11. *Ibid.*, Ch. 43.
12. *Ibid.*, Ch. 37.
13. *Ibid.*, Chs. 20 & 21.
14. *Ibid.*, Ch. 22.
15. *Ibid.*, Ch. 35.
16. *Ibid.*, Ch. 32.
17. *Ibid.*, Ch. 32.
18. *Ibid.*, Ch. 41. 'Mahendra stood near the staircase for some time for a beef-up—he was excited by the love that he bore Binodini and persuaded himself that he had captured the one whom he desired so long, forgetting all the world, so there was no barrier between the two—it was a day of happiness for Mahendra.'
19. *Ibid.*, Ch. 51. "Mahendra's passion increased two-fold. He said with an emotion-choked voice, 'Binod, I was waiting on the bank of the Jamuna, but the moon of the sky informed me that you were waiting for me here, hence I came away.' Saying this Mahendra advanced to place himself on the bed."
20. *Ibid.*, Ch. 51.
21. *Ibid.*, Ch. 45.
22. *Noukadubi*, Ch. 5.
23. *Ibid.*, Ch. 23.
24. *Ibid.*
25. *Ibid.*, Ch. 27.
26. *Ibid.*
27. *Ibid.*, Ch. 30.
28. *Ibid.*, Ch. 35.
29. *Ibid.*, Ch. 30.
30. *Ibid.*, Ch. 61.

31. *Chaturanga*, 'Sachish'/10.
32. *Ibid.*
33. *Ghare-Baire, Sandiper Atmakatha* (Sandip's story). No. 3.
34. *Ibid., Bimalar Atmakatha* (Bimala's story). No. 6.

3

Rabindranath's Concept of World-humanism and *Gora*

The mystique of faith in life and man that led to Tagore's sublimation from humanism to world-humanism was without doubt rooted in his close study of the Upanishads. It was through his father that he came in contact with the Upanishads in his childhood. But that was not much deep because Debendranath's pursuit of the Upanishadic thoughts was a bit hamstrung by his faith in the Brahmo Unitarianism for which he had some difficulty in espousing Upanishadic Pantheism or Sankaracharya's Monism. Still because of his deep reverence for the Upanishads the independent Brahmo method of worship that he formulated embraced some significant Upanishadic messages. 'It was through them that Rabindranath was introduced to the Upanishads in the family prayer meetings in his boyhood. But that connection was essentially external and for this very reason could not influence the thoughts of his later life' (Bandyopadhyay: Mukhopadhyay, 3, translated). The extensive spread of influence of the Upanishadic thoughts that moulded the poet's outlook to life in later years was the result of his close study of and reverence for the Upanishads in his maturer years. The Upanishadic thoughts not only attracted him deeply, but had a great impact on his multifarious activities and thinking, not only in the concept of the Visva-Bharati, but in his concept of world-humanism.

The main source of inspiration for his concept of world-humanism is surely the first *sloka* of the *Ishopanishad* which says:

Isha basyamidam sarbam yatkincha jagatyam jagat (everything belonging to this world is enveloped by God). There is no doubt that Tagore's concept of world-humanism is the result of the conceptualisation of divine presence in everything belonging to this world. Another *sloka* referred to by Rabindranath himself expresses the same idea which shows the depth of his indebtedness to the Upanishads for his concept of world-humanism:

Yastu sarbani bhutani atmanyebanu pasyati
Sarbabhutesu chatmanam tato na bijugupsate.

(One who sees all the living beings inhering in the Supreme Soul and *vice versa* does not hate anybody).

At the opposite pole of Tagore's world-humanism is nationalism which impedes the growth of world-humanism and which divides nations on narrow separatist lines. He was in no doubt that the First World War was, to a large extent, the result of extreme nationalism of Germany. He realised that the Indian concept of nationalism which flourished at the initial stages of the freedom movement was moulded by the European concept. As a counterpoise to this narrow sentiment which fragments the world into small segments by narrow domestic walls, as he says in poem No. 72, *Naibedya,* he favoured the ideal of India's *tapoban* life mode, the life-mode of the ancient *rishis* which was not constricted by narrowness, but embraced everything in its patent expansiveness. To counter this narrow concept of nationalism Tagore wanted an awakening of the spirit of love and man's good sense: 'Therefore man will have to extert all his power of love and clarity of vision to make another great moral adjustment which will comprehend the whole world of men and not merely the fractional groups of nationality' (Tagore: Manna, 386-87).

In order to attain this objective of wholeness and inclusivity the ideal of unity as followed in India is the only ideal. Speaking of the character of unity pursued in India Tagore says: 'Through centuries India has come to lay, with various materials, the foundation of the unity-oriented civilisation which is the ultimate for mankind. She has never cast away anybody as something foreign, has not driven out anybody as non-Aryan, has not ridiculed anything as something incongruous. India has accepted everything, has absorbed everything' (Tagore, *R.R.*, 15; 706, translated).

The quintessence of India's cultural heritage in this principle of absorption of different cultures, as Jawaharlal Nehru has said in *Dynamic Life*: 'The other day I read one of Rabindranath Tagore's poems or rather a translation of it, which spoke of the wonderful variety of India where innumerable streams have flowed, producing the culture we now possess. The capacity to observe these various streams of culture is a part of the creativeness of India.' Inspired by this ideal of unity and cultural absorption that India followed through centuries Rabindranath thought that this country was most favourable for the growth and development of the concept of world-humanism: 'In India the vast problem of the global man will be solved' (Gangopadhyay, 93, cited). It is for this reason that though he was steeped in love for his country, he was inspired by the ideal of world-humanism, and followed it not only as an ideal but translated it into practice. Hence the conceptualisation and establishment of Visva-Bharati, the motto of which is—mirroring the macrocosmic world in the microcosm of a single place (*Visva yatra bhabatyekanidam*).

Though Tagore has articulated his thoughts on world-humanism in poems, essays, songs, so far as the novels are concerned he has expressed his thoughts on the subject only in *Gora*. On the other hand, in *Gora* are also enshrined his thoughts on the soul of India. Everything considered, *Gora* is the mirror image of Rabindranath's mind, and the protagonist Gora, in his love for India, with her weakness and ignorance and superstitions and prejudices, and in his sublimation into the global man, is his spiritual child. Since unity in diversity is the watchword for the socio-cultural history of India through centuries, contrary forces are no destabilising factors in the fabric of life but make a harmonised whole by merging in the mainstream.

In this novel there is a picture of the conflict between the old Hinduism and new-fangled Brahmoism. In the last decades of the nineteenth century there was noticed a dialectical conflict raging in Bengal between the extreme Hinduism of the revivalist Hindus and the extreme Brahmoism of leaders like Brahmananda Keshab Chandra Sen. "The area of dialectical discourses between the ancient Hindu religion and the new-fangled Brahmo religion was marked out and extended and the 'relation' between the traditionalist conservative Hindu society and reform-conscious progressivist Brahmo society gradually soured through animosity and sarcastic exchanges" (Bhattacharya, 323, translated).

All the stumbling-blocks to the marriage between Benoy and Lalita—on the one hand, stiff opposition of the Brahmo society and on the other, Lalita's resistance to Benoy's adoption of the Brahmo religion as a pre-condition for marriage—are removed through the mediacy and firmness of the prejudice-free liberalist Paresh Babu. When even Gora does not come forward to help solemnise this marriage, Paresh Babu bears the brunt of ridicule and even braves the threats of the Brahmo society, yet he does not flinch from what he considers the path of truth—safeguarding freedom of the individual against all odds. He says, 'Truth cannot be tested without conflict and opposition. It is not that truth was tested once and for all to a group of men of high intellectual and spiritual ability in ancient times; truth will have to be discovered in a new light to people of every age through opposition and strike. However, I do not want to enter into any argument over this, I honour freedom of the individual. By striking with that touchstone of individual freedom we come to know correctly what is eternal truth and what is ephemeral fancy—the well-being of the society depends upon knowing it and making an attempt to know it' (*Gora,* 433, translated). Neither Hindu nor Brahmo society has ever crumbled because of this marriage, on the other hand, at the end of the novel Gora goes to the liberal-humanist Paresh Babu accompanied by Sucharita because he is above all religious prejudices, on being awakened to a new truth after learning of the story of his birth. Surrendering to Paresh Babu's liberal-humanist philosophy a metamorphosed Gora says, 'You have the *mantra* of this deliverance. It is for this reason that you have no place in any society. Make me your disciple. Initiate me today to the *mantra* of that god who belongs to all—Hindus, Muslims,

Christians and Brahmoists, the door of whose temple does never get closed to any nation, any individual, who is not the god of the Hindus only, but the god of India!' (*Gora*, 502, translated). That is, eternal humanism is the god of India. Paresh Babu emblematises that truth.

Rabindranath started serialising *Gora* in *Prabasi* (a monthly journal) in 1314 B.S., but actually the incidents fictionalised in *Gora* relate roughly to the year 1882 or 1289 B.S. In other words the events related in the novel have a time-lag of twenty-five years. The patriotic feelings that were aroused in the minds of the people in the last part of the nineteenth century (especially in Bengal) were closely connected with Hinduism. 'Nationalism and Hinduism were almost merged with each other. Rabindranath too seems to have been somewhat influenced by these equational feelings in the first phase of the *Swadeshi* movement. His poem entitled *Sivaji-utsav* carries proof of this. The dream of an undivided India enshrined in the poem is that of a Hindu India. Sivaji fought the Mughal Emperor and established an independent Hindu kingdom, so only the Hindus can feel proud in its glory, not the Muslims. The Sivaji festival is an explicit expression of Hindu nationalism' (Bhattacharya, 322-23, translated). Gora's patriotism is also synonymous with Hinduism. At first Gora is a staunch Hindu—his sublimation to the global man is the result of his final metamorphosis through deeper realisation.

Out of deep love for the country he angrily counters the police officer who has tyrannised over the residents of Char-Ghoshpur (*G.*, 190), has gone to police custody by punching and kicking the constables who have dragged the students to the police station for nursing a wounded Calcutta-based cricket player by soaking shreds of a *chaddar* in a reserved pond (*G.*, 197), and again, opposes his own release from police custody with the help of a lawyer out of sympathy for the poor subjects who cannot do the same for want of money (*G.*, 198). He finds time to visit the houses of the low-caste people even in spite of his tight work schedule because of his love for the country and even acquires the habit of smoking tobacco from a hubble-bubble (*G.*, 107). That this love is synonymous with his Hinduism is proved by numerous activities of his. His pride is in being a native of India with her prejudices and superstitions, customs and traditions, with her good and evil—'My culture lies in accepting and practising what you call superstition. So long as you will not love the country and stand on the same platform with the people of the country, I will not tolerate a single calumnious word from your lips against the country' (part of his argument with Panu Babu, *G.*, 68, translated). In reply to Benoy's arguments in support of his marriage with Lalita he says, 'What pains me is that by marrying a Brahmo girl you want to segregate yourself from the people of the country.... Your love does not lie where my love is. You have no love where you want to free yourself with a knife. There my love is most intrinsic. I want my India—whatever blame or abuse you may hurl at her, I want her and none else; I do not want myself nor anybody else as greater than her. I did not want to engage in any activity which would cause the least separation from her' (*G.*, 342-43, translated). The India he loves he loves in her totality, and in that love his Hinduism is overtly expressed. In his arguments with Benoy he has articulated his sincere love for India which is complete with her superstitions, paganism and caste system. He says, 'I want to share the same seat of humiliation with that India which has been shunned by the whole world, which is being humiliated—this my caste-ridden India, my superstitious India, my pagan India' (*G.*, 343, translated). In support of India's paganism he enters into a discourse with Sucharita on the difference between the Indian and European (Graeco-Roman) forms of paganism. He says, 'In the images of Greece and Rome man's imagination was based not so much on knowledge and devotion as on his sense of beauty. In our country imagination is deeply connected with knowledge and devotion. Neither our Krishna and Radha, nor our Har and Parvati are just subjects of historical worship; they embody man's eternal knowledge of the fundamental Truth. It is for this reason that the devotion of Ramprasad and Chaitanyadev has found expression through these images. When has such a sincere expression of devotion been found in the history of Greece and Rome?' (*G.*, 415, translated). By combining Hinduism with patriotism Gora observes even the most insignificant Hindu rites and customs. Putting the *tilak* on his forehead is the pride of his Hindu ways, his penance for staying in jail is the expression of his devotedness to Hindu customs.

It must be admitted that his narrow Hindu sentiments and equation of patriotism and Hinduism show the narrowness of his mind. He has an illiberal mindset, especially his strong disaffection for the Brahmos showcases his biased attitude, apart from the narrow groove of his thought-processes. 'There is no liberality in this kind of patriotism or worship of the country, no expansiveness of vision and judgment, no touch of the vast ideal of man's nobility, no chance to understand and adopt different ideals' (Ray, 415, translated). Gora's Hinduism is congeneric to the ideal of a united India as expressed in Rabindranath's *Sivaji-utsav.* But 'soon Rabindranath saw Hinduism, India's religion and society, and India's independence with a developed, unprejudiced and universal eye and weaning himself away from the hot field of politics adopted the path of thought and action according to his own ideal' (Bhattacharya, 324, translated). His sublimated transition to a developed unprejudiced universal thinking from the narrow groove of Hindu nationalism was not abrupt but effected through a very subtle and inner process of evolution. In different essays and discussions he highlighted the extension of Hinduism into all-embracing humanism through its newer expositions. In an essay entitled *Bharatbarshia Samaj* (Indian society) written in 1308 B.S. he says, 'The essence of Hinduism is to envision the human society in Brahma, instead of setting up the ideal of self-interest at the centre of human society' (Rabindranath, *R.R.*, 2, 625). For Rabindranath the catalyst of change is the ideal of unity pursued in Indian *tapoban* life or the ideal of oneness. For Gora what catalyses his sublimation from narrow Hinduism to world-humanism is the story of his birth (*G.*, 496). When he learns from Krishnadayal that he was born of Irish parents and that he was brought up in the Krishnadayal family on his mother's death after his birth, then his mind is confounded on the question of identity: "He seems to be floating like a momentary dew-drop on a lotus leaf. He has no mother, no father, no country, no nationality, no name, no *gotra,* no god. Everything about him is 'no'" (*Gora,* 496). Rabindranath's thoughts in the first part of the twentieth century have been thrown back on a novel based on the events of the eighth decade of the nineteenth century and it is for this reason that *Gora* is the mirror-image of Rabindranath's life and mind.

Gora's search for India's true identity or fundamental unity irrespective of her good and bad qualities before his sublimation to world-humanism has an existentialist character. His native and spontaneous love for the country and its people may look narrow and partial, yet the unseemly features of the country's cultural life like superstition, paganism etc. he accepts forcefully like the existentialists who 'give emphasis upon whatever is despicable, insignificant, terrible, horrible and unclean; because it exists....' (Manna, 166, translated). To Gora India's ugliness has a different significance. His love for India in her totality is an ideal of wholeness and in spite of the basic contradiction in his outlook—his bias for narrowness (Hinduism) and love for totality (India in her totality) is a step towards his sublimation to world-humanism. His metamorphosis into a global man is the culmination of the evolutionary process that started with his narrow Hinduism and gradually passed through the love of India in her totality. Not only does he request Paresh Babu to initiate him into liberal humanism, but he is sublimated to world-humanism only after conceptualising Anandamoyee as the very incarnation of *welfare:* 'You have no caste, no custom, no hatred—you are the image of welfare!' (*G.*, 503, translated). Again she is conceptualised as the image of India—'You are my India!' (*G.*, 503). In this way Rabindranath has discovered the source of world-humanism in India's basic pursuit of human welfare. The mother who brings up a child belonging to a foreign religion with the loving care of his own mother and can make all kinds of sacrifice for doing so, is the real source of world-humanism.

Gora's concept of world-humanism which is a replication of Tagore's own—is slightly different from the Christian concept of universalism. It is above all sense of religion, a secular concept and feeling in which caste, religion, nationality—everything is merged to make a greater concept of humanity. Gora's sublimation has been made possible because of his love for all the Hindus, without distinction of caste and creed. He needed only a punch which is provided by the story of his birth and upbringing. *Gora* tells the story of its protagonist's border-crossing.

WORKS CITED

1. Hiranmay Bandyopadhyay in the Introduction to *Rabindrachetanay Upanishat* (The Upanishads in the mind of Rabindranath) by Anilkumar Mukhopadhyay, 1382 B.S.
2. Tagore's essay entitled 'Nationalism in India' cited by Gunamay Manna in *Rabindra Rachanar Darshanbhumi* (The Philosophic Base of Rabindranath's Writings), Papyrus, Kolkata, 1993.
3. Tagore's essay entitled 'Bharatbarsher Itihas' (India's History) in *Rabindra-Rachanabali,* Vol. 15, Visva-Bharati; 1402 B.S.
4. *Rabindranather Chhotogalpa O Upanyas* (Rabindranath's Short Story and Novel), Upendranath Bhattacharya, Kolkata, 1395 B.S.
5. Rabindranath Tagore, *Gora,* Visva-Bharati Granthan-bibhag, Kolkata.
6. *Rabindra-sahityer Bhumika* (Introduction to Tagore Literature), Niharranjan Ray, Kolkata, 1369 B.S.
7. *Rabindra-Rachanabali* (Tagore's Works), Vol. 2, Visva-Bharati, 1402 B.S.
8. Narayan Gangopadhyay, *Kathakobid Rabindranath* (Rabindranath the Story-teller), Kolkata, 1392 B.S.

4

Damini—The Rebel Woman

Connotational device for naming a character is as old as literature itself. Jonson's Volpone meaning 'the cunning fox,' Shakespeare's Malvolio (Mal + volio = 'ill will') and Middleton and Rowley's De Flores (who deflowers the chastity of Beatrice-Joanna, the heroine of *The Changeling*) are but a few illustrious examples to show how flouting the norms of Logic, Proper Names can become connotative. The same semantic formulation informs Tagore's naming of characters like Nandini, Damini *et al.* 'Damini' in Bengali means 'lightning' which she indisputably is, as she exudes the light and heat of the lightning-flash. More significantly, Tagore makes a subtle distinction between 'Damini' and 'Soudamini' which mean the same thing, but this distinction adumbrates a transformation from her rebel self to a far more mellowed manifestation.[1]

First serialised in four consecutive issues of *Sabujpatra* from Agrahayan, 1321 B.S. to Falgun of the same year, as four different stories under four different names, *Chaturanga* (Four Aspects) was first published in book form in Bhadra, 1323 B.S. The publication of the second story in *Sabujpatra* gave a foretaste of the cohesive character of the four stories which its book form fully corroborated. Though Damini is the name of the third part of the novel, which deals with her evolution and development in more specific details, Damini, the heroine of the novel, makes her appearance in the sixth section of the second part, Sachish.

We first see Damini—a widow, but an image of full-blossomed youth burning with the passion of physical desires and eager for enjoying life. In the eyes of Sribilas, the narrator of the novel, 'Damini is, as it were, the lightning hidden within the folds of Sravan clouds. Outside, youth has overbrimmed her physical features; within, flickers of flame are burning scintillatingly.'[2]

In Sachish's measured judgment as engraved in his diary she is the picture of hedonism, one who refuses to deny the pull of youth, denies death, yearns to enjoy life to its dregs[3]—an antipodal refraction to the ways of widowhood. Her philosophy is in antinomial contrast to the defeatist philosophy of meek submissiveness represented by Nanibala (the pregnant woman in the *Jyathamashai* chapter, whom Sachish saves, gives shelter and plans to marry against all social calumnies, but fails because she commits suicide), who dies to pay for another man's sin. Damini turns a rebel after the death of a non-complaisant husband (Sibtosh) who does not care to satisfy her psycho-physical needs during their brief conjugal interlude, on the other hand subjects her to the tyranny of devotion[4] after accepting the discipleship of Lilanandaswami. In fact, steamrolling her sensibilities, he consigns her at death as part of his movable property to his Guru along with all his immovable property.

She is thus a victim of the specific hegemonistic modes through which patriarchal power operates and castrates female subjectivity. The collapse of her father's jute trade and consequent bankruptcy and poverty destroys the possibility of her journey back to her father's home. Repression of her bodily needs by an attempt at forceful initiation to devotional ways keeps them temporarily subdued, but after her husband's death she refuses to drown herself in the 'wave of devotion'[5] flowing in her house at the cost of her own money. She staves off the call of the importunate Guru for giving her counsel, feigning illness. In order to prop up her adevotional image she even falsely says that she went to a theatre show if she is remiss in arranging for the evening assembly of devotees. She thus turns to what Chris Weedon calls 'negative protests'[6] in another context. But her repressed desires do not thrust her into destructive behavioral mould, for she is love-starved and with love, starved of bodily needs and the possibility of a love-relationship with Sachish, tears off her rebel's mask and assumes the graceful persona of surrender. The rebel Damini mellows and becomes 'stable Soudamini'[7] and her adevotional attitude takes an about-turn: the rebel suddenly becomes a pliant devotee. But Sachish fails to pierce through the veil of her outward beauty to reach her mind. Here her revulsion to Guruji's devotional ambit and her attraction to the fold of Sachish's love are neatly expressed by the signifier of the broken photograph of Lilanandaswami in meditative posture.[8] The apt referral of the imagery of fire and lightning in this phase of Damini's transformation is in consonance with her inner flame of desire. She is so extremely actuated by her repressed passion that she is seen by Sachish one calm winter noon after a tiring session of devotional discourse to bang her head on the floor of her bedroom saying, 'Stone, O Stone, O Stone, take pity on me, kill me.'[9]

Bengali novels before *Chaturanga* portray socially proscribed aberrations of Hindu widowhood and their severe consequences: Matangini for illicit sex relationship with Umashankar in Sibnath Shastri's *Jugantar* and Rohini first for illicit love escapade with Gobindalal and then for betrayal and dual loyalty in Bankim Chandra's *Krishnakanter Will* pay the price of their aberrations by their lives. Damini is not a direct descendant of those unfortunate widows, but is a much more developed version of hapless widowhood, reformed and animated because in between there is Binodini (*Chokher Bali*) in this evolutionary process. Damini is much bolder, more introspective and more resilient. In quick pursuance of her new-found passion for Sachish (though unrequited and one-sided) she accompanies the Guruji in his travel to some inaccessible terrain because Sachish is a follower (and Sribilas too). Her abortive adventure into the seaside cave where Sachish is resting in solitude, to receive only his kicks (in exchange of her respectful love-surrender) and break down in tearful retreat, is her moment of truth. For though it causes in her temporary umbrage and pseudo-revulsion for Sachish, it gives her a new enlightenment about life.

In Sachish's experience in the cave in the twilight region of trance and semi-conscious wakefulness the reality of Damini appears as a sort of the Jungian 'shadow,' the shadow of the 'mass of hunger'[10] which perplexes his mind. It is the verisimilitude of an *a priori* fear of lapse from his devotional path (Damini's behaviour, especially her banging the head on the floor, is a veritable cause for fear of destabilisation). But to Damini it is the male animus which brings in its trail umbrage and revulsion, however temporary and feigned as said earlier, towards the object of her love. In her post-cave return to normalcy she channels her love to suffering animals, gets hold of a bruised kite and gives it motherly care and affection and even nurses an ugly pariah puppy. Her equal care for flower plants is cognate with this transference of love. While Adela Quested's hallucinatory experience in the Marabar caves in E.M. Forster's *A Passage to India* shows a 'negative refraction,'[11] Damini in a worse situation develops a positive attitude to life, her umbrage notwithstanding.

Her attention to Sribilas at this point of her life is tangentially correlative to a sort of 'passivity' in respect of Sachish. Sribilas does her errands and gravitates towards Damini, but her relationship with him is at best peripheral, for in spite of the bruise on her breast that Sachish has inflicted in the cave her passion for the latter still remains undiminished. Sribilas' analysis of women's nature in general ('What little I have seen from the surface, from outside, has convinced me that women are ready to give their hearts where they are sure to get suffering in return'[12]) is very appropriate in this context. It is a kind of masochistic pleasure as noted by Helene Deutsch[13] which makes 'the attraction of suffering' a prime urge for giving themselves up to men in a spirit of love-surrender.

Speaking about the genesis of feminine passivity Helene Deutsch links it with 'feminine masochism' and says that they are 'both the outcome of the feminine constitution and of a mechanism of instinctual reversion related to it that turns energies directed towards the outward world inward....'[14] Damini's passivism towards Sachish which is a show of her outer self may be related to this psychologic link with masochism. She demonstrates a pseudo-revulsion for Sachish, yet retains a 'masochistic love bondage'[15] (later elevated to a spiritual plane) with Sachish which is undeniably interwoven with her female psyche. She cannot abandon or have disdain for Sachish for the pain inflicted by him, but in spite of her internalisation of the male animus as noted earlier, which causes passivity in her, she retains her love (elevated from passion) till the end.

Rabindranath here makes a case study of a 'masochistic love bondage' which is often encountered by psychoanalysts and social workers. Ms. Deutsch cites the example of a 'charming young girl' who came quivering to a safety shelter called Hull House with her tear-stained swollen face made bloody from blows from her lover. She was not married with him and received blows from him occasionally. Yet when she recovered a bit, she went back to her place, as she had to clear it for Pierre who was always very weak when he returned drunk. In fact, 'she was enslaved by her masochism, the strongest of all forms of love.'[16]

It is now Sribilas who procures 'modern' books for her, it is he again who brings her a bamboo basket for keeping her mongoose under control. Sachish's unpalatable proposal to her for shifting her to a relative's place because her presence in their midst is an impediment to unhindered pursuit of their devotional life is an added spur for this show of favour to Sribilas (her 'order'[17] to Sribilas to bring her some 'modern' books, for example). Damini's riposte to Sachish's proposal is an indicator of her animus: 'One of your devotees will make an arrangement according to a certain plan, another will make another arrangement according to another plan—am I a pawn in your hands?'[18] Thus the process of destabilisation that has begun in Sachish with the falling off of Damini's rebel mask—her transformation from 'Damini' to 'Soudamini' as cited earlier—has now reached a climactic point: 'Externally Sachish does not default in meditation, worship and discussions, but a close look at him reveals that within him he is losing grip—his legs are tottering'.[19] He makes a desperate attempt to bring his mind under control, goes again to the seaside solitude and returns with a battered body and exhausted mind, while in Sachish's absence Damini too lives in the sequestered world of self-imposed captivity. It is a conditional reflex for a woman who has given her heart to an unbending man, wallows in suffering and yet behaves like the *khandita nayika* (offended heroine) of Sanskrit poetry. Sachish's harshness hurts her, his sweetness soothes. Hence, when the battered figure calls her and invites her to come in their midst and be one with them,[20] the rebel is transformed again, becalmed at the munificent large-heartedness of the man whom she adores. It is a test of fortitude as much for Damini as for Sachish who goes through the contrary processes of distancing from and remaining close to Damini to see which method suits him best to stave off his desire and keep his steadfastness in his devotional path intact. Ever since he has seen the grace of Damini without probing her mind, when passion for Sachish has seized her, *i.e.*, in the first contact between the two, when her hard mask of rebellion falls off,[21] he has been oscillating between control and lapse and his behaviour *vis-à-vis* Damini changes accordingly. His acknowledgement of mistake in asking Damini to leave (as she is a source of destabilisation) and open-arm invitation to her to join them, and Damini's instant pledge of compliance are followed again by a very significant spell of graceful behaviour on the part of Damini, for from this point on she is trying to rise above passion and seek the sublime region of love. Tagore here makes a very subtle distinction between these two states of the same emotion and sets to change the whole contour of Damini's life. The unbearable glare of her mind is mellowed[22] and she becomes an embodiment of devotion in her *tasar* attire and looks fresh as just-bathed. An internal struggle between her devotee self and desire-fixated self peeps through the glint of flame striking out from the corner of her eye in her dealings with Guruji. But howsoever forced, her behaviour has the stamp of sincerity to conquer. On the other hand, Sachish fails to conquer his weakness for Damini, and she becomes such an entity of truth that her image refuses to be suppressed or thrust beyond the boundary of the conscious. Contrarily, it appears with a reality of representment above all the lines of songs and theories of religious discourse.

Damini is salvaged from her spiritual crisis by the death of the wife of Nabin, a member of the *kirtan* party, who marries his wife's guardianless sister after a brief spell of illicit romance and the ugly face of passion and lust catalyses her final transformation. With the death of passion that consumes and the birth of love that ennobles she has no difficulty in accepting Sachish as her saviour Guru:

> "Damini said, 'You become my Guru. I won't accept anyone else. Give me such a *mantra* which is far above all this—by which I can be saved. Don't fix even my god with me.'"[23]

She can now admit love within the parameter of devotion.

The traumatic incident cited above is an eye-opener to Sachish also, but he cannot rise above the dichotomy of his thirst for form (here the beauteous form of flesh) imaged by Damini and his mad pursuit of the formless (here the infinite). However, he finally rises above the subversive pull of Damini by imploring her to leave him: 'Him I am on the look-out for I need most—to the exclusion of everything else. Damini, have pity on me, do kindly leave me.'[24]

The repetitiveness of the same appeal (the first request is made in Chapter 3[25]) has the desired effect on Damini—she leaves for Calcutta accompanied by Sribilas with the fire of doomsday burning in her[26]; but that fire does not consume her, not Sachish either. For soon she consents to Sribilas's proposal for marriage as a recuperative retrieval of her love. But her love takes on a new resonance when she mingles her conjugal love with spiritual love for Sachish. He is the first truth in her life whose kicks-in-the-cave taught her to internalise the futility of passion and primacy of love. That is why, her fatal chest pain is her 'secret wealth,' her 'touchstone'[27] which has made the union with Sribilas possible. She dies with unsatiated desires, but with the feeling that it is not passion that dogs her like Nemesis to death.

Hers is not a circular story of a rebel ending up in destruction, but a linear story of transformation and elevation to a state of sublimity and calm brought about by rejection. Her request to Sribilas to take her to the seaside to die,—because it is the originating locus of her pain—reminds one of the calm mountainside death of Wilson in Somerset Maugham's story, *The Lotus Eater* and has the foretaste of peace earned through rebuff:

> 'অনায়াসে যে পেরেছে ছলনা সহিতে
> সে পায় তোমার হাতে
> শান্তির অক্ষয় অধিকার।'[28]

> [One who can easily bear deception gets the undying right of peace at your hands.]

NOTES AND REFERENCES

1. *Rabindra-Rachanabali* (henceforth referred to as *RR*), Visva-Bharati, 1394 B.S., 442.
2. *RR.*, 440.
3. *RR.*, 440.
4. *RR.*, 441.
5. *RR.*, 441.
6. Chris Weedon in *Feminist Practice and Post-structuralist Theory,* 1992, 114: 'Many frustrated women, trapped within unhappy marriages, turned to negative protests, such as illness.'
7. *RR.*, 442.
8. *RR.*, 442.
9. *RR.*, 442.
10. *RR.*, 444.
11. *E.M. Forster: A Passage to India*/John Colmer, 1969, 61.
12. *RR.*, 446.
13. Helene Deutsch/*The Psychology of Women* (1947), Vol. 1, 216.
14. *Ibid.,* 188.
15. *Ibid.*, 211.
16. *Ibid.*, 212.
17. *RR.*, 451.
18. *RR.*, 450.
19. *RR.*, 450.
20. *RR.*, 452.
21. *RR.*, 442.
22. *RR.*, 453.
23. *RR.*, 454.
24. *RR.*, 462.
25. *RR.*, 450.
26. *RR.*, 463.
27. *RR.*, 466.
28. *Tomar Sristir Path/Shesh Lekha.*

5

THE HOME AND THE WORLD IN THE LIGHT OF TAGORE'S VIEWS ON COMMUNALISM

One of the main strands of thought that characterises Tagore literature is harmony—between man and man, community and community and ultimately, union between the limited and the unlimited. With his message of harmony he travelled all over the world preaching the gospel of world humanism. His *The Home and the World* is an important document enshrining his warning against the danger of communalism.

Though the novel was written at the initial stage of the First World War, its political backdrop is formed of the nationalist movement against the British Imperialist power sparked off by the *diktat* for the Partition of Bengal (1905). This proclamation created a strong resentment in the Bengali mind, which was channelised into various protest movements. Rabindranath associated himself with these protest movements and focused on the need for Hindu-Muslim unity. He composed the famous song, '*Banglar mati Banglar jal*' (The soil of Bengal, the water of Bengal) and also took part in the 'Rakhibandhan' festival in which he prayed for the good of 'the soil of Bengal' along with many important personalities of Bengal at the ghat of the Ganges and tied *rakhi* on the wrist of all, high and low.[1] In the afternoon after the foundation ceremony of the Federation Hall in Calcutta he participated in the procession of a huge number of people that proceeded towards the house of Pashupatinath Basu of Bagbazar. The song that the processionists sang was also composed by him:

> The tighter their knot becomes...
> The more will our bond break.

The more red-shot do their eyes be...
The more will our eyes open.[2]

Rabindranath had little doubt about the need for Hindu-Muslim unity in the interest of the country. The picture of Hindu-Muslim divide that has been presented as the political backdrop of *The Home and the World,* which results in communal riot (the serious head injury that Nikhil gets in an effort to save the honour of the womenfolk of Harish Kundu's household has given the novel its open-ended character) has revealed the depth of his conviction about the harmfulness of this schism in the freedom movement of the country.

That the earnest efforts on the part of the well-meaning segment of the population for the communal harmony against the backdrop of the 1905 anti-Partition movement did not succeed was amply proved by the communal riots that flared up in parts of Bengal in 1906-07: 'The communal riots of 1906-07 are the tragic consequence of the Hindu-dominated movement, and perhaps the immediate cause for the decline of this phase of nationalism.'[3] These riots took place in parts of what is now Bangladesh over nationalist movement and boycott. There is no doubt that the Hindu-Muslim riot that is reported at the end of the novel is conceived on the basis of the 1906-07 riots.

Three factors were mainly responsible for this growth of Hindu-Muslim schism—the instigation and incitement of the Muslim maulavis, 'bhadralok' Hindu communalism and the 'divide and rule' policy of the British imperialists. Though the plan for building the nation on the basis of religion gathered momentum in the next phase of the nationalist movement, from the very beginning the Muslim maulavis instigated divisionism because of their strong religious prejudice. Rabindranath has hinted at the instigation of the maulavis in *The Home and the World.* Nikhilesh has asked Sandip to leave his (Nikhilesh's) 'area' after warning him of the Muslims, because they may bring harm to him under instigation from the maulavis who have come over from Dacca:

My husband said, 'Sandip, I come to warn you.'
Sandip said, 'About the fever of poetry?'

Instead of joining in the humorous discussion my

husband said, 'For some time the maulavis of Dacca have been frequenting the place, and secretly they are trying to instigate the local Muslims. They are resentful of you, and may create some trouble all on a sudden.'[4] (Translated from *Ghare-Baire*)

According to a recent researcher, most often the historians have bypassed the 'bhadralok' Hindu communalism in order to foreground the Muslim communalism of Bengal.[5] Through the entire time span of the 19th-century Hindu revivalism to the anti-Partition movement of the first decade of the 20th century an attempt was made in Bengal to focus on Hindu revivalism and establish a cultured 'bhadralok' image of the Hindu. Without doubt there was an urgent need for breathing a new life into the Hindu religion. It was endangered on the one hand, by the extreme Anglophilism of the newly-educated Bengali youths under the impact of rationalist teaching by Derozio in the Renaissance age (of Bengal), and on the other hand, by the rapid spread of Rammohan-introduced Brahmo religion. So a high-voltage Hindu revivalism was the only recipe for the sheer survival of the religion. In this connection one may refer to "the extreme cultural chauvinism of men such as Pandit Sasadhar Tarkachudamani, which proclaimed the 'scientific' basis of Hinduism."[6] A segment of the Western-educated middle-class Bengalees considered themselves alone as 'cultured.' The 'bhadralok' Bengali mindset that began to develop towards the close of the 19th century was founded on this 'culture.' "Since the late nineteenth century, the bhadralok had regarded themselves as a group that was 'cultured'; by the early twentieth century, they saw themselves, more specifically, as heirs to a particular cultural heritage, the 'Bengal Renaissance.'"[7]

This educated 'bhadralok' Hindu segment of the population took part in the anti-Partition/first phase of the nationalist movement. Not only were they divorced from the Muslim community, they were segregated from the common people also, as a result of which the first phase of the nationalist movement failed to become broad-based or inclusive. The leaders too were a handful of Western-educated Bengalees whose concept of independence was formed by a study of Western literature and Western political philosophy. The fount of thought of such renowned thinkers as Burke, Gladstone, Garibaldi, Mazzini etc. was the source of their inspiration.[8] Rabindranath has focused on this Western-educated self-centred leader class of people through his portrayal of Sandip in *Ghare-Baire/The Home and the World* (his followers are B.A./ M.A. passed or F.A. plucked youths). The fat amount of fifty thousand rupees that he demands from Bimala in the name of the country he seeks to spend not just in the cause of the country but for his personal comfort also: 'At least for once in my life I want to squander fifty thousand rupees in a couple of days for my own comfort and in the cause of the country. I am a lord, casting off this camouflage of a poor man for two days only I would like to see my reflection in the mirror; I have a desire like that'[9] (translated). What Rabindranath wants to show is that this kind of a false patriot is nothing but a self-interested hedonist behind his patriot's mask. Under the leadership of such patriots the freedom movement of the country is doomed to failure. The deep resentment among the Muslims and Sandip's flight from his place of operation are the inevitable results of this false patriotism of the movement's leaders.

In an essay analysing the causes of the failure of this movement Tagore says, "I was involved with the nationalist movement when it came to our country. The Muslims did not take part in it, were opposed to it; some among the leaders angrily said that they should be ignored completely. I know that they did not participate in it. But why did they not? It is really astounding to think of the tremendous cohesion that developed among the Hindus at that time. But such a vehement passion was confined to the Hindus, it did not touch the Muslims! We did not take any lesson even then.... When I first entered the office of our zemindari estate, I saw one day that my chief rent-collector kept a portion of the white sheet on the carpet of the wooden cot removed in his sitting room. When I asked him about the reason, he replied that it was meant for those honourable Muslim subjects (ryots) who were allowed entry into the sitting room. They would have to be allowed to sit on the same cot, yet they had to be made to understand that we were separate from them.... After that one day we have called them to say, 'We are brothers, you too will have to accept loss, to go the way of imprisonment and death.' Then suddenly we find that the 'other' wears the new scarlet fez on his head and says, 'We are separate'"[10] (translated). In *Ghare-Baire* (*The Home and the World*) the Hindu nationalists not only did not make a common front against the British with the Muslims but alienated them by tyrannising over them (the Muslim boatman, for example). More of this later.

One of the important aspects of Hindu revivalism was the awakening of pro-Hindu feelings in the minds of the people. There was an elaborate process of Hindu awakening in Bengal right from the last days of the 19th century, for example, through nationalist activities of organisations and institutions like Hindu Mela, Sanjibani Sabha etc. and such hero-worship festivals as Pratapaditya festival, Sivaji festival etc. These institutionalised expressions of patriotism culminated in conceptualisation of the motherland as goddess (e.g., the motherland as Durga in Bankimchandra's novel *Anandamath: Twang hi Durga dashapraharanadharini*/You are Durga equipped with ten weapons).

Again in order to cope with the dark forces of British imperialism the nationalist leaders worshipped the goddess Kali also, who was power incarnate: 'the principle of feminine strength (Kali) was often evoked in nationalist writing in resistance to the aggressive masculinity of imperial culture....'[11] But "nationalism was generally more comfortable with the manageable, maternal alternative of the goddess Durga."[12]

In *Ghare-Baire*/*The Home and the World* Sandip's preference first for Kali and then Durga as the source of strength reveals a dichotomy which is symptomatic of the nationalist leaders' duality in the choice of the right goddess to invoke in their fight against British imperialism. In the burgeoning relationship with Bimala, when she is struggling to free herself from his snare 'like an ensnared deer'[13] (translated), Sandip plans to worship Kali by idolising Bimala as the goddess herself: 'I am a worshipper of Kali, and one day I shall truly worship her, setting Bimala on her altar of Destruction.'[14] But in a short while he changes his presiding deity and makes an elaborate arrangement for worshipping Durga in league with

Harish Kundu.[15] That Rabindranath did not support this equalisation between the country and the goddess (either Durga or Kali) is evident from the account of the ideological conflict between Sandip and Nikhilesh. In the opinion of Sandip, 'There will be no awakening in the country unless people have a visual image of the country before them. The country therefore needs the image of a goddess'[16] (translated). But Nikhilesh considers it nothing but a false infatuation. Arguing against Sandip's concept of the 'political goddess,'[17] Nikhilesh emphatically comments, 'The country is not the goddess.'[18]

In this novel Tagore has portrayed the anti-Hindu feelings of the Muslims (e.g., the Hindu-Muslim riot), instead of cooperation and integration in the nationalist cause. There are very cogent reasons for the disaffection of the Muslims, a significant one being the casualness with which they were called to join the movement, as Sandip says, 'Our work has now taken a very positive form. Our party has secretly spread itself far and near. We have cried hoarse calling the Muslims as brothers to come and join us, but we have at last understood that it is not at all possible to bring them into our fold by persuasion. They will have to be thrust to the bottom; they should know that power lies with us'[19] (translated). Sandip's words sound haughty and divisive, neither conciliatory nor integrative.

The British imperialist forces were greatly responsible for fanning this divisive passion among the Muslims. The British rulers' divide-and-rule policy was aimed at creating hatred among the Muslims against the Hindus. The British foisted an upper-caste character upon the national movement and propagated the theory that the movement was an attempt by high-caste Hindus to establish control over the body-politic. In the infamous Rowlatt Committee Report the 'bhadralok' identity of the terrorists of Bengal was emphasised. 'As soon as the national movement entered the phase of mass struggle in 1905, the colonial administrators, ideologues and publicists began to portray it as a Brahmin and upper-caste movement whose objective was to substitute the benevolent British rule with tyrannical upper-caste rule. The fact that Ranade, Gokhale, Tilak, Aurobindo Ghosh, Lajpat Rai, Mahatma Gandhi,

C.R. Das, Motilal and Jawaharlal Nehru, Sardar Patel, C. Rajagopalachari, and Subhas Bose were upper-caste by birth was held out as proof of the theory of the upper-caste character of the national movement. Similarly, the infamous Rowlatt Committee Report emphasised the Bhadralok Character of the Revolutionary Terrorists of Bengal.'[20]

There can be no doubt that the disaffection caused by the tyranny over the poor Muslims (and even Hindus like Panchu) by the *Swadeshis* (Hindu) that has been portrayed in the novel in the context of the boycott of foreign goods and bonfire of British clothes had the instigation of colonial administrators. Lord Curzon himself went to Dacca to tell the Muslims that the creation of East Bengal as a separate province would pave the way for Muslim domination over it.[21] The sporadic incidents of communal riots that took place in parts of East Bengal over *Swadeshi* movement and boycott were alleged by Muslims to be the result of interference by the Hindus (*Swadeshis*) over their free choices. They were being forced to purchase coarse indigenous clothes and salt and dirty sugar instead of fine British-made clothes and white British salt. The government propaganda singled this out as the direct cause of riots.[22] The examples of *Swadeshi* tyranny that Tagore has cited in the novel are the sinking of Mirjan's boat for bringing British clothes to the village *hat*,[23] and arranging for realization of money from a poor Muslim by forcing him to marry off his young wife.[24] In another instance cheap German shawls were forcibly burnt from a poor farmer.[25] As this incident is cited in the context of the failure of the *Swadeshis* to bring the Muslims under control, the poor farmer may be presumed to be a Muslim.

All these inevitably lead to the failure of the nationalist movement as suggested by the flight of Sandip and communal riot (as a result of which Nikhilesh receives a serious head injury). Rabindranath was never in two minds over the need for communal harmony in the greater interest of the country.

At the end of the novel Nikhilesh rushes to save the women of Harish Kundu's household from indignities at the hands of the Muslim rioters,[26] which is prompted by his liberal humanism. What is important to note here is that Harish

Kundu is no friend of his, but an enemy. In this respect his predecessor is surely Gora (the hero of Tagore's novel of the same name), who is elevated to a greater concept of humanism above narrow Hindu sentiment. Tagore was stirred to the thought of union between man and man after coming out of the eddy of the division of Bengal.[27] Gora and Nikhilesh are the most meaningful products of that salubrious thought-process.

NOTES AND REFERENCES

1. *Rabindrajibani*, Prabhat Kumar Mukhopadhyay, 2nd Vol., 1368 B.S., 139.
2. *Ibid.*, 140.
3. '"I will make Bimala One with my Country": Gender and Nationalism in Tagore's *The Home and the World*,' paper by Indrani Mitra in *Modern Fiction Studies*, Summer 1995, 244-45.
4. 'Bimala's Story,' *Ghare-Baire*, Visvabharati, 1991, 162.
5. Joya Chatterji/*Bengal Divided*, Cambridge University Press, First Paperback Indian Edition, 1996, 152.
6. *Ibid.*, 156.
7. *Ibid.*, 155.
8. *Sahitya-Bichitra*, Rathindra Nath Roy, Jijnasa, Calcutta, 1964, 175-76.
9. 'Sandip's Story,' *Ghare-Baire*, 121.
10. 'Swami Sraddhananda,' *Rabindra-Rachanabali*, Vol. 12, Visva-Bharati, 1402 B.S., 658-59.
11. "I will make Bimala...."/Indrani Mitra, *MFS*, Summer, 1995, 256.
12. Tanika Sarkar in an essay entitled "Nationalist Iconography" etc. published in *Economic and Political Weekly*, 21 Nov., 1987, 2011-15, cited in Indrani Mitra's essay "I will make Bimala....", 256.
13. 'Sandip's Story,' *Ghare-Baire*, 83.
14. *The Home and the World* (translated version of *Ghare-Baire* done by Surendranath Tagore), Macmillan, 1992, 107.
15. 'Nikhilesh's Story,' *Ghare-Baire*, 165.
16. 'Sandip's Story,' *Ghare-Baire*, 125.
17. *Ibid.*, 127.
18. *Op. cit.*
19. *Ibid.*, 124.
20. Bipan Chandra, *Essays on Contemporary India*, Har-Anand Publications, 2nd ed., 1999, 63.
21. *Oupanyasik Rabindranath* by Dhirendra Debnath, 231.
22. *Rabindrajibani* by Prabhat Kumar Mukhopadhyay, 2nd Vol., 172.

23. *Ghare-Baire,* 118.
24. *Ibid.*, 134.
25. *Ibid.*, 117.
26. *Ibid.*, 206.
27. *Rabindrajibani,* 147.

6

A Feminist Approach to *Yogayog*

> Love was the most ancient of all the gods and existed before everything else, except Chaos, which is held coeval therewith.... The summary of collective law of nature, or the principle of love, impressed by God upon the original principles of all things, so as to make them attack each other and come together, by the repetition and multiplication whereof all the variety in the universe is produced, can scarce possibly find full admittance in the thoughts of men, though some faint notion may be had thereof.
>
> —Francis Bacon, *The Wisdom of the Ancients*

This epigraph from Bacon which prefaces the poems of the Australian feminist poet Judith Wright's *Woman to Man*[1] sums up the Elizabethan philosopher-writer's notion of primacy given to love in the scheme of creation. Judith Wright, on her part, not only proclaims the indispensability of love in procreation and continuity of life on earth, but identifies love with 'the life-force, the great creative and unifying force of the universe.'[2] In the following extract from *Woman to Man* Wright scripts the history of the birth of child as the product of love-sublimated sex:

> 'This is no child with a child's face;
> this has no name to name it by;
> yet you and I have known it well.
> This is our hunter and our chase,
> this third who lay in our embrace.'

The poem gives utmost importance to the woman in the act of creation:

'The eyeless labourer in the night,
the selfless, shapeless seed I hold,
builds for its resurrection-day—'

and concludes with an image of love embrace that is vital for continuing the life-process:

'Oh hold me, for I am afraid.'

Rabindranath's *Yogayog*[3] (Communication) portrays a clash between two antipodal concepts of marital love and sex as represented by a commercially successful wealthy merchant—Madhusudan and a finely-tuned sensitive 19-year old woman—Kumudini nurtured on the Hindu ideal of womanhood and traditional concept of wifehood. In Madhusudan's concept of marital relation with wife there is nothing as love, fine sense and sensitive behaviour, for he understands sex as realizable by force. The wife is the symbol of captive sex which can be exacted by authoritarian force. She is nothing but another item in the inventory of his possessions. His idea of the woman has been moulded from a very narrow mercantile vision: 'Madhusudan has seen women very briefly among the daughters-in-law of the house. They perform the daily chores of the household, engage in quarrels, whisper family secrets to each other, and even shed tears over trifles. In Madhusudan's life there is little contact with them. He never thought of anything better than an insignificant slot of this world for his wife, but rather thought that she would lead a zenana life under the silent command of the menfolk's eyes behind the boundary wall shadowed by the littleness of the daily household routine. It did not occupy the slightest space of his account-sharp careful brain that there was an art in behaving with the wife, that there might arise a difficult problem about gaining or losing something in it' (997).[4]

This attitude to women in general and wife in particular explains the series of his rude behaviour to Kumu starting from his marriage with her. This also explains his concept of procreation: 'There is only one way to tie Kumudini to his own life in a tight knot, and that is the way of making her the mother of his child. He finds consolation from that imagination' (1010). The difficulty of having sex with his newly-married wife and her carefully calibrated distancing from him from the very first night of their union force him to consider the meanest of the ways for forging dominance over her.

This is a far cry from the husband-wife-child trinity as conceived by Judith Wright of which the child is the culmination of sex-love between the husband and the wife. So in Madhusudan's mercantile concept love is non-existent, the wife is a commodity for sex-gratification and the child is a means of punishing a recalcitrant woman named wife. However at the end of the novel when Kumudini is reported to be pregnant, he takes her to his home with a show of pomp and power, possibly on the twin grounds of subjugating a wayward wife and giving continuity to his lineage.

If Madhusudan's commercial mindset is the product of a steadfast and unwavering pursuit of wealth, Kumu's romantic mindset is the product of her childhood loneliness, her eldest brother Bipradas' influence and her close initiation to the classical heritage of India: 'Bipradas has a deep devotion to the Sanskrit literature: Kumu has learnt from him grammar with an undivided attention. Ever since she studied *Kumarsambhab* she visualized Lord Siva in her worship of the deity as the hermit of hermits who was the most desired object of Uma's *tapasya*. In the meditated image of the maid her future husband appeared with the blazing glory of divine sacredness' (979).

Before her marriage with Madhusudan she has formed her mind with such a steadfastness of devotion that the object named husband becomes an impersonal idea to her and irrespective of any lacuna that may be found in Madhusudan the individual, her surrender to the meditated husband-image remains unquestioned (987). But the ground reality after her marriage throws everything out of gear and an unmitigated process of disillusionment sets in which leads to sex repulsion and revulsion for the man himself.

A number of traumatic events brings about this transformation. The brusqueness with which Madhusudan proposes that the *kushandika* ceremony (accepting the bride as wife by giving vermilion mark on the parting of hair by performing *homa*) will be held at the bridegroom's house contrary to custom is the first important eye-opener for Kumu.

Madhusudan's conduct just before and at the time of marriage, especially his deliberate intention to dishonour and lower the prestige of Bipradas because of an old rivalry and quarrel between the two families does not augur well for a happy wedded life for her. Then comes the sapphire ring episode in which Madhusudan forcibly takes away the most prized ring from her on the journey home, because sapphire has an evil association for him. This he does in a way as to establish his authority over his new acquisition that is his wife. All these instances of Madhusudan's rudeness have started in her ripples of discontent which result in the most unusual incident for a new bride about to have consummation of marriage—the swooning (1005). The accumulated insults hurled at her revered godlike brother have pushed her in the opposite direction. Sex-love as celebrated in the above-mentioned Judith Wright poem is impossible to develop in such a mortifying situation. The process of sex repulsion has started when she feels targeted by a bird of prey: "Kumu's heart went shivering just like the female pigeon's seeing the shadow of the hawk from the sky. Her cold hands were sweating, pallid was her face. Immediately after coming out of the room she held the hands of Moti's mother and said, 'Take me to a secluded place for some time. Let me alone for ten minutes'" (1005). When ultimately Kumu comes into Madhusudan's room, the latter greets her with another bout of acrimonious attack upon her and her brother which causes deep resentment in her. The night of consummation of her marriage teaches her some hard truths in respect of her husband's meanness, inferiority complex *vis-à-vis* Bipradas and the incompatibility of their marital relation.

It is however in the next morning's discovery of the loss of her ring that makes her realize her servile status in her husband's home as she inconsolably asks Moti's mother: 'Let me ask you one question, will there be nothing to call my own from today?'(1007). It is servility that she has been consigned to which is impossible for her to digest because her study of the Sanskrit classics and epics has taught her the equality of status for the wife. This feminist agenda of the novel is kept up throughout except at the end when

Rabindranath seems to retreat bowing to social conventions and mores.

Kumu's stand-off is determined by the behaviour of her husband as she says to Moti's mother, 'See, sister, I came to give myself up to him, but he did not allow me in any way. Let him remain with the maid-servant. He will not get me' (1008). She gets another reminder of her non-identity in the household when Madhusudan castigates her for giving Hablu a glass paper-weight (1009). Her silent revolt against the authoritarian hegemony of her husband and the subversion of her independent identity and rightful status of equality takes the form of self-ostracism. She takes refuge in the small room for storing oil lamps adjoining the main store room. This serves her the twin purposes of saving herself from the ignominy of submitting to the loveless lust of Madhusudan and protesting against the rank denial of self-esteem and individuality. Madhusudan oscillates between command and entreaty for the sole purpose of sex-gratification. In order to win over Kumu's mind so that she submits to him Madhusudan brings in Nabin and Moti's mother to Kumu and revokes the order given to them earlier to go to Rajabpur and engages them in her service. He stoops to his unaccustomed low to conquer his wife, for he cannot wait any more (1032). This lowliness of Madhusudan creates insoluble problems for Kumu, for she can cope with a rough and insolent Madhusudan but fumbles for a solution when he is meek and mild. To the deceptively mild yet inexorable call of Madhusudan to come to his bed her reply is, 'I am not yet mentally prepared. I crave for some time' (1034). But ultimately she has to submit to his sex hunger and invite him to the bed. This is a tragedy for her from which even her god cannot save her. This surrender to the sex hunger of a loveless, insensitive husband is nothing but molestation of her womanhood. It is a triumph for Madhusudan, but what a triumph! Rabindranath here makes the uncharacteristic authorial comment on Kumu's defeat and Madhusudan's triumph: 'But can it be called a triumph?' (1036), thus giving Kumu's tragic narrative a monologic character. The occasional cry of a tethered dog coming from outside piercing the silence of the night against which this tragedy is being enacted only images the agony of an incarcerated Kumu.

This fictive reality of loveless sex has a close resemblance to the real-life tragedy of a similar kind of a latter-day Indian feminist poet Kamala Das for whom marital love is a much-craved-for but elusive reality. "The love that she receives from her husband is nothing but 'an empty gift,' 'a gilded/ empty container, good for show' ('Captive'...). She, therefore, asks her woman-persona as under:

> Woman, is this happiness, this lying buried
> Beneath a man?
>
> ('The Conflagration'...)"[5]

In another poem, titled 'Forest fire' she speaks blatantly of sex-hunger which is most uncommon for an Indian poet because it is against Indian custom and culture:

> 'Of late I have begun to feel a hunger
> To take in with greed, like a forest-fire that
> Consumes, with each killing gains a wilder,
> Brighter charm, all that comes my way.'

The articulation of this 'hunger' is not only anti-cultural, but this 'hunger' is intemperate and all-consuming and hence harmful. 'The discontent in love at the legitimate source is definitely responsible for this condition of hers, and through the poet-persona the whole Hindu social set-up comes in for a sharp criticism. In this rotten set-up, marriages are made without taking into account the suitability of the partners from various angles—their family back-ground, age, education, financial status and social connections. Kamala Das raises her voice of resentment against this hollow set-up...'[6]

Kumu rebels against the mismatch by dissipating her soul: 'Does the call that she accepted as divine consist in this unholiness, this internal unchastity? Has the god enticed the victim because he wants woman sacrifice; will he take an offering of the lump of flesh, that is the body which is bereft of the mind? Today the feeling of devotion could not be aroused by any means. So long Kumu has repeatedly said, You bear with me—today the rebel's mind says, How can I tolerate you?' (1036) She cannot say of the child born out of such loveless lust—'This is our hunter and our chase,/the third who lay in our embrace' like the speaker in the above-mentioned Judith Wright poem. It is not strange that Kumu's sudden knowledge about her pregnancy at the end of the novel does not send any exhilaration in the recesses of her mind, though motherhood is supposed to be the culmination of womanhood, as Tagore himself believed once.[7] As a matter of fact the novelistic discourses in the last two decades of the 19th century hinged on this thought: "Pregnancy and motherhood are a major element in the representation of female characters in nineteenth-century fiction, and in the 'Woman Question' novels of the 1880s and 1890s will be the index of recuperation into the prescribed female role—a kind of salvation through motherhood—or of irrecuperability."[8] But whether the motherhood resulting from 'legalised rape'[9] which occurs in the case of Kumu is welcome is debatable. For a loveless sex-relation Kumu has a strong revulsion: 'Kumu has such a strong revulsion for the sweaty touch of one whose power of control is so slack, whose love belongs to the same class as material attachment' (1037).

A couple of incidents which aggravate Kumu's bitterness and widens the breach between Kumu and Madhusudan involve Hablu, Madhusudan's only nephew, and bearer named Murali. The child is the only source of consolation to her, on whom she lavishes all her affection. She finds utmost joy in his company as it soothes her tortured soul. In one of the incidents Madhusudan snatches away most rudely from Hablu's hand the handkerchief containing flowers given him by Kumu herself and then forcibly takes away from Kumu a paper wrap containing cardamoms given her by Hablu. So shocking is Madhusudan's behaviour that it simply stuns her (1040). In Murali's case it is Kumu's offer of an old wrapper which complicates matters (1049). In both instances Madhusudan makes an insolent show of his wealth to compensate for the denials. But Kumu realizes how limited her area of freedom is in the household and how mean and narrow-minded her husband can become.

Madhusudan makes some mawkish attempts to please Kumu, for example, by his return of Kumu's sapphire ring (1051) and gifts of her favourite *esraj* and pearl necklace (1054). These bribes and lollipop inducements are but poor compensation for the space of harm already inflicted and make little dent in her wall of disjunction. Kumu realizes the impossibility of establishing love relationship (which of course involves sex) with Madhusudan but then considering that it is a great sin to fail to surrender her mind and life to her husband she should at least make a recuperative attempt to behave as Sati and Sabitri (1053). She imploringly tells her husband to make her his own—to give her punishment. A lean chance for a temporary truce is lost when Kumu makes a very light and insignificant prayer for helping Murali. Madhusudan comes with a bounty of wealth but Kumu reciprocates with a scant prayer (1055). Kumu's bounteousness in a scant prayer is beyond the obtuse ken of a wealth-centred vision. Madhusudan's attention to Shyamasundari, his widowed sister-in-law at this point of the husband-wife incompatibility is significant, for after Kumu's departure, which takes place very soon, from his house, he engages in blatant and unabashed acts of adultery with Shyama which may spell disaster for Kumu as Moti's mother realizes (1067).

In Bipradas' Calcutta house where Kumu goes to see her sick eldest brother, but actually to escape from an untenable existence with Madhusudan, she learns of his adultery and resolves not to go back to her husband's house, as she tells Madhusudan (1093). But to Bipradas who has already learnt of this illicit affair (1081), it is an affront to the womenfolk in general and so he incites her to wage a war on the society which is very niggardly in giving the woman her due (1082). He too is at first positively against sending Kumu to Madhusudan's house. He says to Moti's mother, when she comes to see Kumu and advise her to return to her husband's house, that it is another man's house, not Kumu's own, and so she cannot stay there (1083). But the picture changes suddenly when Kumu's pregnancy is ascertained. This is a stunning knowledge for Kumu, for the very brief familiarity with her husband has created a distorted image which becomes very distinct to her mind at the apprehension of pregnancy (1097).

The novel ends with Madhusudan's triumph over a recalcitrant wife by posting her with great fanfare to his Mirjapur palace. Before leaving for her husband's house bowing to social convention Kumu for once burns with the anger of protest: 'But one day I will free them, make myself free too;

come back I will, you will see. I cannot live in falsehood being false. I am the seniormost mistress of their house, what meaning does the position have if I fail to become Kumu?' (1099).

The nature of the conclusion of the novel dilutes its feminist agenda, for it is abrupt, fortuitous and against the grain of the story. The woman who wages a relentless, albeit silent, war against the erosion of honour and assault on individuality has to surrender to an uncalled-for motherhood. Madhusudan takes home the phallic woman because the question of continuing his lineage is involved with it, thus giving the novel a phallogocentric character.

There is an aporia embedded in the abrupt end of the novel. The conclusion exemplifies the way in which a feminist discourse which begins on a strong anti-establishment note is diluted into a conservative one and consigns the woman to her familiar psychological stress under which she passes the best moments of her married life. The hapless Kumu is shown to be trapped in gestation and childbirth which do not result from sex-love. The patriarchal familial oppression is likely to be re-enacted as there is no way for self-determination for Kumu found explored. In her poetry Judith Wright gives special emphasis upon sexual love, for it is the force which has the power to defeat death and time. "Her manifesto—'I am the maker'—does not simply apply to the poet as 'maker,' it is also a recognition of the power of sexual love to transmit life through time."[10] This metaphysical possibility of sexual love is irrelevant in Kumu's case, for sexual love is non-existent in her life. The sex-hunger of Madhusudan that results in Kumu's pregnancy will continue his lineage but given Kumu's attitude to unwanted pregnancy, it is not known whether the mother-child relationship will ameliorate her condition and give her empowerment.

Recent feminist studies focus on the importance of 'women's mothering' and the effect it has, especially its social implications, on producing "a fundamental structure of expectations in women and men concerning mothers' lack of separate interests from their infants and total concern for their infants' welfare."[11] But the way Abinash Ghoshal, the scion of the Ghoshal family is felicitated on his 32nd birthday at the start of the novel (969) and the way this is linked to an account of the Chatujye-Ghoshal old rivalry stress the patriachal character of the discourse. Kumu and her mothering remain in the shade.

NOTES AND REFERENCES

1. Vide *The Poetry of Judith Wright* by Shirley Walker, Edward Arnold (Australia) Pty. Ltd., 1980, 91.
2. *Op. cit.*
3. *Yogayog* was serialized in the monthly journal named *Bichitra* from Aswin 1334 B.S. to Chaitra 1335 B.S., for the first two months as *Tinpurush* and the rest as *Yogayog.* It was published in 1336 B.S. Vide *Rabindrajibani*/Prabhat Kumar Mukhopadhyay, 3rd Vol., 1961, 336.
4. Figures in brackets refer to text page numbers. Text used is *Yogayog* in *Rabindra-upanyas-samgraha,* Visva-Bharati, 1990. All translations from the text of *Yogayog* are by the author.
5. *Kamala Das and Her Poetry* by A.N. Dwivedi, Doaba House, Delhi, 1983, 91.
6. *Ibid.*, 31-32.
7. *Rabindranather Chhoto Galpa* by Pramathanath Bisi, 1392 B.S., 119.
8. *Thomas Hardy and Women* by Penny Boumelha, 1982, 59-60.
9. Citing Rabindranath's own remarks in this regard as made in a letter to Radharani Devi, dt. 14 Bhadra 1335 B.S.—'Such a huge humiliation is equal to adultery—it is as it were an insult to the god—submerging in mire what is best in you'—Prabhat Kumar Mukhopadhyay writes in *Rabindrajibani,* Vol. 3, 1961, 339: "The situation in which Kumu became pregnant is in a way 'legalised rape' by another name."
10. *The Poetry of Judith Wright* by Shirley Walker, 1980, 33.
11. *Feminist Practice* and *Post-structuralist Theory* by Chris Weedon, Blackwell, 1992, 60.

7

The Gender Question in Tagore's Last Novels

the palm goes
always to the light;
who most shall advance the light—
call it what you may!

—William Carlos Williams

Gynocentric discourse claims to be reaching out towards the light—more freedom and empowerment to the women are the only objective. While feminist critics in general questions the traditional male and phallocentric ideologies, Hélène Cixous, the exponent of *écriture feminine* dispenses with biological determinism in *The Laugh of the Medusa* (1976) and asserts that 'women often write in male discourse and men can write in a feminine way' (Cuddon, 267). As a matter of fact, there is a section among the feminists themselves who tend to give credence to the fact that male representations of women are not as insignificant as thought in radical criticism.

Seen in the light of this condescending acknowledgement of male discourse of women, Rabindranath Tagore's representation of women is pre-eminently feminist, especially in the post-*Sabujpatra* phase of writings. Tagore is not a feminist by label, but has always advanced the light in matters feminine. Society's centuries-old conservatism which dies hard against change is attacked in his writings at the slightest opportunity and his writings—all genres—mirror the condition of women who live in the male-dominated patriarchal society in a marginalised state. In one of the early short stories—*Denapaona* (Dowry)—Tagore has shown the travails and tribulations of a girl who has not brought sufficient dowry to her husband's home. Even in a subsequent story called *Haimanti* the girl of the same name dies a slow death only making a firm protest.

But Rabindranath was not only naturally sensitised over the plight of women in Indian society, he wanted to establish the individuality of women because it is individuality which ensures dignity, self-respect and sexual independence of women. 'From the very beginning of the twentieth century Rabindranath internalised the newer complexities, various ideas and currents of thought of the social life of Bengal. There were already signs of the break-up of the large Bengali joint families and community life; it is not very difficult to notice its shadow in Bankim's novels. Those signs assumed a more distinct shape. Sense of individual identity became firmer; there developed a need for determining the individual's relation with society. But all this was confined to the handful educated people of the middle class; for...it was this class in the greater Bengali society which was the herald of social progress and manipulator of social ideas and concepts. It did not take long for Rabindranath to make an objective analysis of these newer and more complex social problems....' (Ray, 404, translated).

Rabindranath advanced the women's cause by positing a new iconography of rebellion in the epoch-making short story *Streer Patra* (The Wife's Letter), published in *Sabujpatra*, Sravan, 1321 B.S. issue, in which Bengal's first rebel woman, Mrinal, flees from an incarcerated existence in her husband's house into individuation and freedom. *Sabujpatra* is really the watershed in Tagore's concept of women's empowerment. Never before does a Tagore heroine make bold to flee from the institutionalised bond of the home (in-laws') to freedom and being. This representation of a housewife taking a desperate step which drew vehement criticism from the conservative section of society is a bold construct that had more to do with the discovery in the West of the dignity of woman as woman irrespective of her value in different roles—mother, daughter, wife. Socio-economic changes in the West which transformed people's outlook on life also spawned fresh thoughts on the question of the emancipation of women. The Suffragette movement at the beginning of the twentieth century reinforced the campaign for women's rights in the West. While

Rabindranath valorised women's individuality ever since he wrote *Chokher Bali* (The Eyesore), he oscillates between traditionality and bold unconventionality on the gender question especially in his novels from *Chokher Bali* onwards.

Mrinal's (*Streer Patra*) realisation of the futility of an incarcerated life in her husband's house and her leaving the security of the institutionalised relationship remind one of Ibsen's Nora who also leaves home in search of the self:

> *Helmer.* Haven't you been happy here?
>
> *Nora.* No, never. I thought I was, but I wasn't really.
>
> *Helmer.* Not...not happy!
>
> *Nora.* No, just gay. And you've always been so kind to me. But our house has never been anything but a playroom. I have been your doll wife, just as at home I was Daddy's doll child (Act 3).

Though Rabindranath had a strong dislike for Ibsen's play in his early years, as a crusader for individual freedom Nora is a fitting predecessor of Mrinal.

Bimala's (*Ghare-Baire*/The Home and the World) return to her husband and home from her husband-engineered freedom of *going out* is on the trail of tradition and Kumudini's (*Yogayog*/Communication) forced return to her husband's house smacks of phallogocentrism but their individuality and Damini's (*Chaturanga*/Four Aspects) strong sense of freedom prepare the ground for the presentation of women in Tagore's last novels—*Dui Bon* (Two Sisters), *Malancha* (The Flower Garden) and *Char Adhyay* (Four Chapters).

Individualism is the marker for Labanya of *Sesher Kabita* (The Last Poem) and though published in the same year as *Yogayog*, the former presents a contrastive discourse on the gender question. While Kumu has to capitulate to the social convention and go back to the loveless house of a peremptory husband because she carries his child, Labanya believes in and practises self-determination. In a poem written at about the same time Rabindranath echoes the silent anguish of Kumudini over the circumstantial constraints frustrating self-determination:

> Why shall you not give the woman
>   Her right to conquer her fate, O God?
>
> ('Sabala'/The Strong Woman, in *Mahuya*, translated).

On the other hand, by declining to marry Amit and selecting a lesser-grade Shobhanlal as her husband Labanya not only prioritises pragmatism but proves herself to be a worthy descendant of Damini in self-determinism.

His last novels are gender-specific and if in *Dui Bon* Sharmila's (the elder of the two sisters) motherly persona is juxtaposed with the beloved-self of Urmimala (the younger sister), in *Malancha* Niraja's frantic but futile endeavour to retain her authority and primacy in the house and the flower garden is portrayed. *Dui Bon* is however a theory novel which is built upon the two-women theory—mother and beloved, as Rabindranath clearly states at the beginning of it:

> Women are of two classes, such a thing I have heard from some scholars.
>
> One class is chiefly mother, and the other beloved (Tagore, 1177, translated).

In her mother persona Sharmila, at least in the initial stages of the novel, is allowed the absorptive role of the all-controlling woman, and hence empowerment. Her ubiquitous presence and control in husband Sasanka's life make her position as woman unique in the sense that as wife none of Tagore's women before her—Asha (*Chokher Bali*), Bimala (*Ghare-Baire*) or Kumudini (*Yogayog*)—has any control over her husband (Mahendra, Nikhilesh, Madhusudan respectively). Tagore's mother Sarada Devi lived in the shadow of the towering personality of her husband. So Sharmila's ubiquitous control (before her illness of course) over Sasanka with the 'ever affectionate care' of a mother beyond the traditional role of the wife is a latter-day concept with Rabindranath reinforced by the developments on the question of women's emancipation in the West. Sharmila's control is evident everywhere—'In the world of her husband's life there is no distant periphery where the control of her kingdom is slack' (Tagore, 1177, translated). Sasanka's delay in returning home from an invitation by friends is not at all brooked by his ever-caring wife with equanimity, for she sends the faithful servant Mahesh, lantern in hand, not only to demonstrate her displeasure, but to escort him back home through darkness (1177). Most important surely is her influencing him to leave his service because of injustice in matters of promotion and accept her proposal to go into the contractor's business on a partnership basis with a distant relative (1179-80).

This mother-image of Sharmila however is neutralised as the novel progresses into the bare complexities which crop up as Sasanka first seeks to drown himself in his world of action and then in his overtly expressed love for Urmila, who is inducted into the household to help in domestic management because of Sharmila's illness. In fact in order to prioritise the ideal mother-image in a wife, *i.e.*, to flesh out an idea Rabindranath has prioritised self-denial as the basic trait in Sharmila's character. On the other hand, Sasanka abhors being tied down to the apron-strings of his motherly, though devoted, wife. He has been portrayed as a man who 'does not at all like to give himself up to the fondling care (of his wife),' but wants to 'get his wife as wife' and seeks 'the pleasure of companionship' (Tagore, 1304, translated). In other words, though Sharmila's control over her household and husband at the beginning of the novel makes her a representative of the empowered women, the picture is diluted in the later phases with her emergence as a failed partner in Sasanka's life, because she cannot satisfy his psycho-physical needs. The self-denying mother in Sharmila learns to digest neglect with equanimity which subverts her strong-woman image. At least on two occasions—Sasanka's birth-day (1182) and their marriage anniversary (1206)—his absence (deliberate?), on the pretext of pressure of work on the former occasion and going on an outing with Urmila on the latter casts her in the shade and leaves her languishing in semi-concealed self-pity.

In her excessive concern for the well-being of her husband Sharmila develops a myopia to the growing intimacy between her husband and her sister, which can be explained only in terms of her self-effacing motherliness. However, the ultimate discovery of this intimacy and a grim realisation about the impossibility of her recovery from illness prompt her to contemplate tying up the knot between her husband and her sister (1206), which does not take place because she recovers and Urmila leaves for England for medical studies.

Of the three patterns of marital relationship delineated in *Anna Karenina* Tolstoy has set up the Levin-Kitty relationship as the ideal because Kitty is not only her husband's partner in love but also in the life of action. Sharmila's graduation at the end of the novel to ideal wifehood—'Explain your work to me, train me, educate me so that I can be a fit partner of your work' (Tagore, 1208-9, translated)—approximates Kitty's sharing of her husband's work, but is actually modelled on the character of Tagore's own Chitrangada who seeks to combine partnership in her lover's love life with partnership in his life of action.

Tagore has not only sought to foreground the mother-image of Sharmila and build her character on the theory of the motherliness of wife, he has also sought to theorise on the irresistibility of the pull of love in life and man's inevitable biological attraction to woman for psycho-physical satisfaction. And this is done through the Sasanka-Urmila relationship which grows in inverse ratio to the husband-wife relationship partly because of Sharmila's incapacity to meet Sasanka's psycho-physical needs on account of her ingrained motherliness on the one hand and illness on the other and partly because of Urmila's finding the meaning of life in biological determinism. She is lively and buoyant and vibrates with youthfulness and love. After the experience of an infructuous relationship with Nirad who bores her by giving moralistic advice to desist from various allurements, she gives full rein to her vivacious self when she free-mixes with Sasanka on being inducted into his household to take charge of it because of her sister's illness. Her release from a life of constriction into the ambience of her brother-in-law's loving companionship gives her independent spirit the right impetus for enjoying life.

Urmi is no Binodini (*Chokher Bali*) who does not mind wrecking Mahendra-Asha's conjugality out of jealousy. So what strikes one in this portrait by Rabindranath is that she does not feel any compunction to wreck her own sister's married life by free-mixing with her brother-in-law. Rabindranath has here created a woman who, starved of psycho-physical satisfaction through her would-be husband (Nirad), wants it in full measure from Sasanka whose happiness in her contact makes her happy (1195). She is never remiss in her duties to her sick sister (1204), yet when Sasanka professes love to her—'You know for certain that I love you; and, for your elder sister, she is a goddess. I do not in my life have greater reverence for anybody else. She is no creature of this earth, she is far above us' (Tagore, 1205, translated)—she makes no protest which means acquiescence.

The confession of Sasanka, on the other hand, though innocuous, borders on a kind of perversion, because it smacks of self-interest, which is found by Freud among modern men who are mostly Oedipal: 'Should the woman of their sexual choice resemble the mother even partially, such men experience psychical impotence. To avoid such humiliation they lower their estimation of the sexual object of their desire and reserve for the mother the overestimation normally felt for their chosen sexual mate. Having degraded their sexual partner they feel free to release their locked up sexual drive which frequently turns out to involve what Freud considers a perverse element of sexuality' (Finney, 24).

However, the object of Sasanka's sexual choice—Urmi—is awakened to a sense of never-achieved responsibility at the end of the novel when she leaves for England for medical studies realising the extent of damage she has done to the family. Once again Tagore has established the independent spirit of Urmi.

If *Dui Bon* focuses on the mother-image of the woman, *Malancha* (The Flower Garden) focuses on the beloved-image. And in this sense *Malancha* is complementary to *Dui Bon* at least theoretically. Though not spelt out in so many words, here Togore has experimented with the woman's beloved-self.

Niraja, the heroine of the novel, is the very embodiment of love, but she is so possessive that she cannot tolerate the presence of a rival in her husband's love for her. And the main focus of attention in the novel is the intensity of her love for her husband.

Another, more interesting, aspect of the manifestation of her love is her love for the flower garden of the family, as she says to Sasanka, 'Ever since after my marriage I learnt that your garden was as dear to you as your life, I did not keep any division between the garden and myself. Otherwise I would have engaged in a fierce quarrel with your garden, I would not tolerate it. It would have been my rival. You know how I have absorbed it in me. I have completely identified myself with it' (Tagore, 1227, translated).

However, this identification of Niraja with her husband's garden is tangential compared to Liubov Andryeevna's (in Chekhov's *The Cherry Orchard*) identification with her ancestral cherry orchard, for while in Niraja's case her love for and identification with the flower garden is co-extensive and synonymous with her love for the husband, in Liubov's case the cherry orchard, especially in bloom, is symbolic of hope and reorientation. The orchard, when awash with the white wave of floral beauty in the spring season, embodies Liubov's dream of a better, more meaningful and less fractured life in her tragic and chaotic spell after her husband's death. She is so absorbed in the existence of the cherry orchard that she 'can't conceive life without the...orchard, and if it really has to be sold, then sell me with it' (Act 3). There is an aesthetic dimension to Liubov's attachment to the orchard: 'All, all white! oh, my orchard!' And she finds something angelic about this beauty: 'After the dark, stormy autumn and the cold winter, you are young and joyous again; the angels have not forsaken you!' (Act 1) Niraja's attachment to the flower garden too has an aesthetic dimension: 'Just as one living abroad eagerly waits for letters on special mail days, from season to season they (Niraja and husband Aditya) have waited for according amassed welcome to different trees' (Tagore, 1213, translated).

If the cherry orchard has a symbolic significance for Liubov, Niraja's love for the flower garden has a different dimension—it is closely linked with her love for her husband.

To her the garden is symbolic of her control over her limited world. She is an active partner in her husband's love life as also the life of action, an enthusiastic co-worker of her husband in the nurture of the garden (1213). So she is deeply agonised when in her illness she finds that for assisting in the work of the garden a distantly related sister of Aditya, Sarala has been inducted into the household (1214). For a time she tries to assert her rights by asking Sarala not to enter the orchid-house and when it fails because Sarala has Aditya's confidence, she argues with her husband, sometimes persuasively, and sometimes hotly, not to allow Sarala to do any work in the orchid-house. 'Still I say, that orchid-house is yours and mine, Sarala has got no right there' (Tagore, 1226, translated), she tells her husband in a last-ditch, agonised effort to retain her rights. Her garden fixation has an ontological correlative in love for her husband which she can never lose by any means. She is the embodiment of jealousy *vis-à-vis* Sarala because in the enfeebled state of her illness she lives under the constant fear of losing her husband's love to her rival. Her persuasion of her husband to marry Sarala off with Ramen and even persuading the latter to marry her is a ploy to get her out of the way. Yet she is torn between a lucid desire for acceptance and a contrary feeling of rejection of the inducted woman. In the last phase of her agonised life Niraja is actuated by a passionate desire to perpetuate her presence in her world—with her husband and in the garden because both are correlated to each other: 'I will stay, I will stay here, I will stay with you, as I visualise clearly' (Tagore, 1243, translated). This is a metaphysical realisation which disarms her, albeit temporarily, of her jealousy for Sarala. Yet in her final moments when she straightens up to utter words of strong rejection seeing Sarala touch her feet ('Get ye gone! hence! at once, or I'l pierce my dart in your breast, I'll dry up your blood'—Tagore, 1244, translated), the vehemence of the reflex action shows the one-track mind of the beloved type of woman who wants to retain full control over her small world of domesticity.

Sarala on the other hand represents another side of the beloved type of woman. Rabindranath has cast her in the determinist mould and hence she does not baulk at reviving the long-suppressed childhood romance with the now-married Aditya, given the first opportunity. She is an emancipated woman and yet is neither irresponsible nor reckless. In spite of her love-relationship with Aditya and Niraja's jealousy for her, she is always alive to her duties to the sick woman.

But the basic ingredient of her character is determinism which manifests itself in her dual love-relationship with Aditya and Ramen and more significantly, in her active participation in the freedom movement. Rabindranath's active support for the participation of women in the freedom movement takes on a more definitive shape in the case of Sarala who goes to jail for committing a serious offence against the British administration. With the emergence of the individualised, emancipated women, they responded to the need for participation in patriotic activities, though risky. Sarala stands midway between an idealistic Bimala (*Ghare-Baire*) and a daring Ela (*Char Adhyay*/Four Chapters), a fit product of the more liberal times.

Ela in *Char Adhyay* (Four Chapters) is again a determinist who is averse to marriage in her early years so that she can chalk out a course of independent life. Through her Rabindranath has presented the picture of an individualistic woman who comes out into the outside world to taste of independence. She is the representative of the educated women who were coming up, though in limited numbers, to plunge into the vortex of the life of action especially in the country's cause and in this sense she is a herald of the new age, as Indranath, the leader of the revolutionary group, acknowledges when she comes to see him for a gainful job. Her unfamiliarity with Indranath does not deter her from making the request (1249). Under Indranath's inspiration she takes a vow of lifelong spinsterhood and devotes herself to the work of the country.

But while making an exploration of individual personality Rabindranath makes Ela highly susceptible to love and shows through a study of Ela's individualistic and independent spirit love's irresistibility. In fact the last three novels of Rabindranath are built, among other things, upon the theory that love is irresistible. While the love of Sasanka and Aditya are socially unsanctionable and has the potentiality of tearing apart the texture of domestic life bringing tragedy in its trail, the love of Ela is also unsanctioned because of her no-marriage vow. But what is most distinctive about this love of Ela is that it is woman-initiated. However there is a contrariety in Ela's attitude in the sense that while marriage is abhorred as at the beginning, love is a manna and like Shakespeare's Rosalind she falls in love at first sight. "For a long time I had been looking at you (Atin) sitting at a corner of the deck (of the ship). I forgot to notice if anybody else was noticing it. It was the most wonderful one-glance introduction in my life made permanent. My mind said, 'From where did this far-away type of man come, who was not made in the mould of his surroundings, but was a hundred-petalled lotus in the midst of moss? Immediately I vowed to myself that this rarity of a man has to be drawn, not just to me, but to all of us'" (Tagore, 1263, translated).

Love makes Shakespeare's heroine adventurous, Rabindranath's adventurous and reckless, as evidenced by her journey to the secret den of Atin (1274). Through love her woman's persona has manifested itself in an ever-radiating glory of womanhood. She surrenders herself to Atin first when he says, 'At heart I am a man, barbarous and wild...' (Tagore, 1269, translated) and again when, at the end of the novel, he comes to kill Ela under instructions from the leader for the safety of the party. That is, she surrenders herself when Atin is most harsh and cruel. Rabindranath has always stressed the fact that however independent-minded they may be, it is in the nature of women to be attracted to men who are wild, brutish and manly.

In his rejoinder to the storm of criticism that raged over the reference to the Roman Catholic-Vedantist-turned terrorist, Brahmabandhab Upadhyay in the Introduction to the novel and the portrayal of Indranath in the mould of a terrorist, Rabindranath highlighted the Ela-Antu (Atin) love story as the only focus of attention, undercutting the discourse of revolutionary activities of Indranath and his men (1306). The text is not structured in a crime-and-punishment frame for Ela's deviation from the no-marriage vow made to Indranath is not treated as perjury and so not punished as such. The end of the novel registers the culmination of the process of Ela's metamorphosis, that starts with her first encounter with Atin, into the eternal woman who seeks to unite with the object of her love in body and mind in life as also in death: 'I am yours, yours completely—even in death. Take me. Do not allow dirty hands (of the police) to touch me, this body of mine is yours' (Tagore, 1288, translated).

WORKS CITED

1. *The Penguin Dictionary of Literary Terms and Literary Theory*, J.A. Cuddon, 1991.
2. *Rabindra-sahityer Bhumika* (An Introduction to Rabindra Literature), Niharranjan Ray, New Age Publishers, Kolkata, 5th Edn., 1369 B.S.
3. Rabindranath Tagore, *Rabindra Upanyas-samgraha*, Visvabharati Granthanbibhag, Kolkata, 1990. Figures within brackets indicate page marks.
4. Anton Chekhov, *The Cherry Orchard.*
5. Penguin *Critical Studies: Sons and Lovers*, B. Finney, 1990.

8

RABINDRANATH'S *SWADESHI* THOUGHTS IN HIS NOVELS

Gigantic insult
Drinks the blood by sucking from
    the breast of the weak
Through million mouths.
    Selfishness-bloated
Injustice derides suffering; terror-struck
Shrunk slave hides in disguise!

—Tr. by the author

Written in 1300 B.S., *Ebar Phirao Moray* records the anguish of Rabindranath at the process of dehumanization that set in in society at large as a result of the tyranny of the foreign ruling class. The apolitical poet saw with severe mental pain how a whole nation was losing its vitality under the oppressive rule of the British. He knew that the road to salvation lay not in the weak-kneed politics of pleas and appeals as pursued by the Congress, nor in the fancy politics as pursued by drawing-room loquacious politicians, nor in the murder-assassination politics as pursued by the terrorists, but in the awakening of love and reverence for the country, in rural reconstruction and in constructive activities.

Rabindranath was not a political man in the sense that Aurobindo Ghosh, Brahmabandhab Upadhyay, Barin Ghosh and others were; he was not even a leader in the sense that Keshab Chandra Sen was. He did not enter into the vortex of politics or social turmoil as his compatriots did; but that did not prevent him from raising his voice against the social and political injustice perpetrated in the country, against the schism and disharmony obtaining among communities, against the blind passion for imitation of the British and crooked kowtowing of a section of his countrymen to the British rulers. He noticed how a blind passion for imitation of the British bred the rabid virus of hatred for the country and voiced his protest against it in poems, essays, articles, stories and novels. His essays give a whole phalanx of his *Swadeshi* ideas that were gradually shaping up in his mind from the last decades of the 19th century onwards. For example, the essays published in *Bharati* of the 80s spoke of the need for self-reliance and denigrated political agitation as 'mendicancy,' while other essays and collections of essays shed light on other strands of his *Swadeshi* thinking. In *Swadeshi Samaj* (1311 B.S.) he spoke of the need for canalizing the force of the movement through constructive work, while in several essays of the anthology, *Raja O Praja* (1315 B.S.) he spoke of the contempt in which the British rulers held this country and sought remedy for it in our attainment of 'manhood' through proper education. He was deeply hurt at the disharmony among the two main communities—Hindu and Muslim and so in the essay captioned *Byadhi O Pratikar* published in *Prabasi* (1314 B.S.), he said,—'In our society there is an evil in respect of the relation between the Hindus and the Muslims, which has been with us for a pretty long time. We have no escape from suffering its consequences.' The British rulers took advantage of this ingrained schism and the result was division of Bengal. Hence his grand conception of a united India in which races merge into one and divisions are blurred:

Come O Aryan, come Non-
    Aryan, Hindu and Muslim,
Come today ye Englishman, ye Christian.
Come ye Brahmin, purifying thy
    mind take the hands of all.
Come ye fallen, remove all the
    burden of your humiliation.
Come without delay into the coronation of the Mother,
    for the holy pitcher is yet to be filled
With the water sanctified by the touch of all—
Come to this grand sea-shore
    confluence of the Indian people.

(*Bharattirtha*, tr. by the author.)

His novels—three out of twelve—*Gora, Ghare-Baire* and *Char Adhyay,* faithfully mirror his *Swadeshi* thinking as much as his essays. But before going into the novels proper, it will be useful to have a look at the socio-political background of the times in which these were written.

Background

The time-span between 1870s and 1910s saw diverse trends on the socio-political scene of Bengal. In the last half of the 19th century, especially when Keshab Chandra Sen's propagation of Brahmoism was in the ascendent, Hindu revivalists became active in order to counter the onslaught of the nascent Brahmoism. Slowly this Hindu revivalism evolved into Hindu Nationalism as British oppression and tyranny were on the increase.

Inspired by Bal Gangadhar Tilak's organization of Ganapati and Sivaji festivals, the Hindu revivalists of Bengal introduced Sivaji festival, Pratapaditya festival etc. It was an age of blind Nationalism in the wake of the British policy of the division of Bengal. Patriotic feelings were roused to a high pitch—through songs, lectures, plays (Girish Ghosh's *Chhatrapati Sivaji, Sirajuddaula* etc., D.L. Roy's *Mebarpatan, Pratapsingha* etc.), through inspiring writings in journals like *Sandhya* (Brahmabandhab), *Bandemataram* (Aurobindo), *Jugantar* (Barin Ghosh and others) etc. and even through unity efforts between communities.

But the movement for rescinding division of Bengal (1905) that created such fume and flame did not follow an politico-economic line as it should have. On the other hand, it based itself on the Hindu revivalist line, resulting in alienation of Muslims, creation of the Muslim League by the efforts of Sir Salimullah and other Muslim leaders of the then East Bengal in 1906 and Hindu-Muslim riots.

The middle-class Bengali Hindus had a respectful attitude to the British in the 19th century, but the division of Bengal angered this section of the Bengalees and hence this movement. Quite naturally the movement for rescinding the division of Bengal snowballed into direct action, but it had severe limitations, for:

(i) it was not all-pervasive, as it was limited to the intellectual and middle-class Bengalees,

(ii) it took the form of militant Hindu Nationalism,

(iii) it alienated the Muslims and

(iv) it gave birth to such exhibitionist-adventurist activities as boycott, bonfire of foreign linen, terrorism etc.

Rabindranath initially welcomed the *Swadeshi* movement in the heyday of the stir against the division of Bengal. His enthusiastic association with the *Rakhi-bandhan* festival (tying the knot of friendship) and espousal of the revivalist cause (he composed the famous poem *Sivaji-Utsav,* when Sarala Debi organized 'Sivaji festival' in Calcutta in 1904) are evidences of his early enthusiasm. But with the drift of the movement into 'extremism' and militant Hindu Nationalism, the essential lacunae of the movement became clear to him and he felt disenchanted with it. He began to think instead if Hindu Nationalism could be made to transcend into Universal Humanism. He advocated self-power, constructive patriotism and union of the masses. 'The only purpose of political pursuits is to unite the heart of the country,' he said.

The Novels

The three novels—*Gora* (1910), *Ghare-Baire* (1916) and *Char Adhyay* (1934)—published within a space of 25 years epitomize his *Swadeshi* ideas as outlined above.

Gora—the magnum opus which mirrors the socio-cultural scenario of the late 1870s and early 1880s, especially the schism between Hinduism and Brahmoism, the narrow sentiments of the Hindu revivalists and mean sycophancy of the educated segment of the society—is a history of the evolution of Rabindranath's own *Swadeshi* thoughts. For Gora's transition from narrow Hindu Indianism to a grand concept of Universal Humanism reflects the evolution of his creator's own thought-processes.

The period in which *Gora* is set was not convulsed by political agitation. Its salient leitmotifs were sycophantic attitude of the so-called educated Hindus to the British rulers, combined with a low, disrespecful attitude to their own country and countrymen, their crass imitativeness and schism between

Hinduism and Brahmoism. *Gora* reflects all the diverse trends of the times, but it may be conjectured that the communal disharmony of the times when *Gora* was written had influenced Rabindranath greatly in portraying the age of the novel. That is, the mind of Rabindranath of the first decade of this century was projected into the times of *Gora* and he sought a solution to the fissiparous tendencies of his own times in the grand conception of Universal Humanism that is the message of *Gora*.

At the initial stages of the novel, Gora envisions a Hindu India, in defending which he is prepared to go to the last limit of his strength and wisdom. He writes articles to counter the attacks on the Hindu *Shastras* and Hindu society by an English missionary and is locked in wordy duels with the Brahmo Panubabu to establish the supremacy of the Hindu religion. He supports the customs and practices of the Hindus because they are part and parcel of his country's culture, while holding the Brahmo in contempt because he is a renegade and divisionist. When the sycophantic Bengalee gentleman travelling first class in the steamer derives pleasure from the miseries of the poor, Gora does not let him go easily and when Panubabu decries the national character of the Indians, Gora espouses the cause of the pagan India riven by casteism, plagued by superstitions. There can be no doubt about the depth of his love for his country. His patriotism is paramount and unquestionable. He goes to jail opposing the tyranny of Government officials on the villagers of Char-Ghoshpur and does not appoint a lawyer to defend his case, because the majority are too poor to appoint lawyers to defend theirs. He takes it as personal loss when Nanda falls a victim to superstition and says in a voice choked with pain and emotion: 'The death of my Nanda at the hands of exorcists hurts me, hurts my whole country.' The idealistic image of India that Gora had formed in his mind gets a big jolt when he sees with his own eyes the misery and distress of the people of Char-Ghoshpur and the unenviable condition of the prejudice-bound rural Bengal.

Rabindranath knew that without village reconstruction no improvement of the country was possible. He translated his ideas into practice in his own limited way and within his zamindar's estate of Silaidaha encouraged cooperative and multi-crop farming, urged villagers to set up schools and build roads, divided the *Parganas* into *mandals* and entrusted their administration to local bodies and set up central bodies for rural administration etc. His agriculture-based work at Sriniketan is common knowledge. Indeed self-reliance and rural reconstruction were his prescriptions for development instead of boycott of British goods and terrorism as pursued and propagated by the political leaders of the 1905 vintage.

But Gora's patriotism moves within the parameters of Hindutva and Hindu India concept, which is partial, not complete. For turning it into a whole, he needs a new realization which comes with the revelation that he is no Hindu, that he is born of an Irishman. At this moment of revelation a new vista of truth unfolds itself before him, for he realizes that "he has no mother, no father, no country, no race, no name, no *gotra,* no god. All his existence is reduced to a 'no.'" In that state of a strange nothingness Gora rushes to Paresh Babu and explaining everything submits to him to initiate him into a new Universal Humanism which admits of no discrimination in respect of caste, creed or religious belief: 'Today you initiate me into the worship of that god who is worshipped by Hindus, Muslims, Christians, Brahmos and all—the doors of whose temple are never closed to any race or any individual,—who is not the god of the Hindu only, but the god of India.' He now has no hesitation to be united with Sucharita in marriage, for he knows that being moulded and brought up on Paresh Babu's ideals, she will be a good partner in his service to his country and that his patriotism will assume a complete shape in unison with her.

Ghare-Baire, written six years later mirrors the political turmoil of the post-1905 period and contains Rabindranath's disapproval of the agitational drift in politics and his espousal of constructive activities. Boycott of foreign goods, bonfire of British-made linen, terrorism, communal riots, dacoity in the name of the country etc. combined to make the movement against division of Bengal a sensational affair which smacked of adventurism. Rabindranath lamented that such a great fund of patriotic fervour as was created on the occasion of the1905 stir were frittered away along destructive channels. He advocated the correct path of constructive activities like the setting up of indigenous business and industrial estates and as already said, rural reconstruction. In place of the terrorist cult which resulted in murder and assassination he opted for Universal Humanism, instead of the boycott movement with its inevitable fall-out of communal riots he opted for harmony. As believed by Nikhilesh's preceptor, Chandranathbabu, politics *sans* humanism is a package of evil and cannot usher in human welfare.

In this novel Rabindranath has propagated the need for strengthening the economic foundation of the country through constructive activities in order to achieve freedom. That is why, instead of supporting the excitement-generating politics of burning foreign linen, Nikhilesh, the novel's hero, opts for setting up bank, industry and launching *Swadeshi* shipping lines. The bonfire of foreign linen may have a sensational and adventurist value, but it also proves oppressive for the small traders like Panchu. On the other hand, Sandip, though not an exact replica of a terrorist leader, carries the stigma of agitation and terrorism and his exposure and transformation show the length to which excitement-generating drama-packed politics could go.

The evil effects of terrorism are portrayed in *Char Adhyay* written 18 years after *Ghare Baire*, in the clearest terms. Though Rabindranath heaped eloquent praise in his essays in *Kalantar* on the bold revolutionary youths of Bengal who suffered untold pain and misery in the cause of the motherland, he could not support terrorism by any means. In *Ghare-Baire* the disapproval is not so pronounced as in *Char Adhyay.* He shows here how the terrorist path ends up in the destruction of one's nature, personality and individuality. The individual is lost being crushed by the faceless cruelty of a difficult mission. The hero Atin laments this crushing of individuality when he confesses to Ela, his beloved-cum-comrade, that he has killed his nature, his individuality. The love between Atin and Ela flounders on the rock of an unbearable immobility of the self which is a prisoner of a wrong faith. The pursuit of a wrong political creed—terrorism—haunts them like Nemesis and Ela has to pay the price for their mistake with her life.

When Rabindranath wrote this novel, Bengal was passing through a phase of revolutionary-terrorist politics. This and the fate of the saintly Brahmabandhab Upadhyay who embraced the revolutionary ideal, repented and confessed to Rabindranath that he had 'a great fall' (as referred to in the Preface to the first edition of the novel) prompted him to write on the evil effects of revolutionary terrorism. Rabindranath's judgment on the revolutionary terrorist politics that his contemporary young revolutionaries followed may be found to be wrong in retrospect. Revolutionary movement of which terrorism was an unavoidable offshoot had a historical necessity. Yet in evaluating Rabindranath's objection one must keep in mind the fact that his finer sensibilities revolted against murder of every variety—whether of an individual or of individuality. A votary of creativity, he advocated instead creative work—rural reconstruction and associate activities. Had the political leaders of the revolutionary India paid attention to socio-economic programmes, independent India would have been far less impoverished.

INDEBTED TO

1. *Gora, Ghare-Baire* and *Char Adhyay* by Rabindranath Tagore.
2. *Oupanyasik Rabindranath* by Dhirendra Debnath, 1384 B.S.
3. *Rabindranather Chhotagalpa O Upanyas* by Upendranath Bhattacharya, 1395 B.S.
4. *Rabindra-upanyaser Prasangik Jignasa* by Smaran Acharya, 1986.
5. *Bangla Upanyas O Rajniti* by Najma Jesmin Choudhury, 1983.
6. *Rabindra-sahityer Bhumika* by Niharranjan Ray, 1369 B.S.
7. *Samaj: Pragati: Rabindranath* by Kshudiram Das, date of publication not mentioned.
8. *Paschimbanga,* special Rabindra Number, 1396 B.S.

9

THE MALE CHARACTERS IN TAGORE'S SHORT STORIES

The plethora of multi-dimensional studies of Tagore's women in the entire length and breadth of his literary works has left his male characters in the shade. Whether it is the near-catastrophic image of Binodini (*Chokher Bali*/The Eyesore), the self-effacing motherly image of the fatalist Dakshayani (*Taraprasanner Kirti*/Taraprasanna's achievement), the early sensualist and later love-composed Damini (*Chaturanga*/The four aspects) or the anti-Establishment bravura image of Mrinal (*Streer Patra*/The wife's letter), or the silently rebellious image of Anila (*Poila Nambar*/The number one), the reader/critic has felt attracted to study the evolution of Tagore's thoughts on, and attitude to women, while it is the male characters who contribute to or help fashion, willynilly, the socio-familial constraint under which the women live and therefore they call for a close in-depth study, especially for their roles in shaping the destiny of the women.

Tagore's writings, especially the fictional and short story parts of them, teem with people of various hues, of homogenous nature and contrary attitudes, of strong mien and weak standpoints. There are egregious women and indifferent men, loving wives and careless husbands, surrogate mothers and over-anxious fathers. They make an interesting picture of different shades.

It must be conceded however that Tagore's short stories have a feminist tilt: it is the problems—physical, mental, circumstantial—confronting the women in their respective situations that claim the largest share of Tagore's attention. They are the warp and woof of a majority of his short stories, the men lending their bit to the final direction their stories take, happy or otherwise.

Some of the stories which have a clear gender orientation are (a random sampling is attempted): *Ghater Katha* (The tale of the ghat), *Denapaona* (Dowry), *Taraprasanner Kirti* (Taraprasanna's achievement), *Kankal* (The skeleton), *Jibita O Mrita* (Alive and dead), *Jayparajay* (Triumph and defeat), *Subha* (Subha), *Mahamaya* (Mahamaya), *Madhyabartini* (The in-between girl), *Shasti* (Punishment), *Samapti* (The end), *Khata* (The exercise book), *Anadhikar Prabesh* (Trespassing), *Didi* (The elder sister), *Manbhanjan* (Breaking the ice), *Dristidan* (Restoring the eyesight), *Nashtanir* (The broken home), *Haimanti* (Haimanti), *Bostomi* (The Baishnav woman), *Streer Patra* (The wife's letter), *Aparichita* (The unknown woman), *Tapaswini* (The ascetic woman), *Poila Nambar* (The number one), *Rabibar* (Sunday), *Musalmanir Galpa* (The tale of a Muslim woman), *Laboratory* (The Laboratory) *et al.*

Men play crucial roles by their positive/negative/indifferent approach to the problems treated. They make or mar or change the direction of the life-pattern of those who come within the ambit of their activity. Or again, their indifference or maladroit handling of situations or inability to measure up to the gravity or combined force of the turn of events or events as they appear spells doom for themselves and others.

The male characters that Tagore has created in his short stories are diverse, varied and multi-hued and of the different categories that they offer we may confine our study to the following to relate their roles to the complications that arise in the story in question:

(i) strong-willed personalities

(ii) weak-kneed cowards/prejudice-bound/nincompoops/ unassertive/compromising/hesitant retreaters

(iii) indifferent husbands

(iv) loving husbands

(v) lovers: indifferent/sensual/Platonic/sincere.

Not all of them belong to the same age-group. There are young, middle-aged, and old people some of whom are protagonists, others subjunctive, while some others are just carry-on lug-boats.

The most important peculiarity of Tagore's short stories is that the characters are culled from the socio-domestic milieu and not from the political arena, and so the men are identified in terms of interpersonal relationships. They are either brothers, fathers, husbands, lovers.

Among the young men who show strong determination and unbending mental strength are very few, microscopic minority, who stand their ground against the onslaught of age-old customs and so-called tradition. The society of which they are members is the patriarchal feudalistic society of the Middle-age variety in which the mercurial father and tongue-lashing mother rule the roost, because unlike the present-day nuclear husband-wife-one child family structure, the structure of their families is uni-cultural, monolithic and top-heavy because undivided. Yet in this close-knit joint family system observing its unwritten laws, maintaining hoary, albeit unethical traditions (unethical compared to today's democratic, scientific and free culture norms) dissenting voices are heard that speak against the peremptory attitudes of authoritarian fathers. Such a dissenter, a young man, a representative of the rising generation, is Hemanta of *Tyag* (Abandonment) who refuses to submit to the set patterns of casteism. His is a solid bedrock support to his lower-caste wife Kusum because he places love above parochial societal norms.

Again the sound of slippers was heard. Harihar Mukherjee came near the door and called out, 'Much time has elapsed, I can allow you no more time. Kick out the girl from the room.'

As soon as Kusum heard this voice, she pressed Hemanta's both legs with double urgency for a lifetime fulfilment of desire in one single moment, kissed his feet, took the dust off them on her head and let them go.

Hemanta rose up to his father and said, 'I'll not abandon my wife.... I do not observe caste prejudice.'

Then you too get out (Translated).

Similar is the robust stand taken by Bibhuti, the groom in the story *Yagneswarer Yagna* (Yagneswar's ceremony) who protests against the flagrant waste of *chhana* supplied by Yagneswar to the members of the bridegroom's party when his stock of foodstuffs meant for them is washed away in rain. The young man comes up and reprimands his father for the wastage of *chhana* by the members of the groom's party.

Bibhuti said with emotion-choked voice, 'Father, what sort of behaviour on our part is this?' Saying this he took up a dish containing *chhana* and began serving it to the men and directed the milkmen, 'Stand at the back, if the *chhana* is thrown into the slush, it will have to be retrieved and served again.'

A stray member or two hesitantly looked at the face of Goursundar to leave eating if they could.—Bibhuti said, 'Father, you too get down to eat, it is quite late in the night.'

Goursundar sat down to eat. The *chhana* began to reach where it should (Translated).

Even in the post-colonial India bride-burning and tyranny of the in-laws over dowry and that of bridegroom's men over the bride's father at the time of marriage show a steady upward trend and Tagore's recipe seems to be to rouse the conscience of the younger generation against such tyranny which is a degrading relic of a feudalistic past. The courage of the young men of Hemanta's ilk saves life and ensures conjugal happiness.

In a rare instance of courage and straightforwardness Sambhunath Sen, father of a would-be bride, Kalyani (*Aparichita*/The unknown woman), teaches the shameless specimen of a groom's dowry-hungry guardian (the maternal uncle) the right lesson by refusing to give his daughter in marriage to the groom because he (the maternal uncle) examines the accuracy of the weight of the would-be bride's ornaments. In a pejorative go-by message Mr. Sen, the harried father of Kalyani, says, 'I can't give my daughter in marriage to a family which thinks that I have stolen my daughter's ornaments.'

Dowry is a very much real concomitant of the marriage process in the present as much as it was in the past societies, and protest must come from within the family set-up, not from the Women's Lib crusaders/social workers alone for its eradication.

A votary of truth and self-righteousness like Mr. Sambhunath Sen, Ramkanai, the old beleaguered husband and maladjusted father in *Ramkanaiyer Nirbuddhita* (The folly of Ramkanai) upholds justice and truth in the forgery case against his own son by giving evidence in favour of his widowded sister-in-law who gets her dead husband's properties—movable and immovable—as decreed in the latter's dying will.

It is another kind of boldness on the part of a young man which saves the fledgling conjugal life and love of Apurba-Mrinmoyee in *Samapti* (The end). Apurba's intelligence and bold handling of a wild girl-wife establishes her to her responsible self and sets her firmly on the threshold of a burgeoning romance.

The reverse pictures, that is, of weakness, cowardice and a gawky inactivity are many and the men's inaction even against strong provocations leads to the ruin of personal happiness and conjugal propriety and results in death and tragedy. The most remarkable is the inaction and retreat of the husband of Haimanti (*Haimanti*) who fails to stand up to the mercurial obduracy of his father as he refuses to send her with her father. When his father-in-law is humiliated by his father and Haima's mind is turned into stone, he attempts a feeble salvage operation, pleading with his father to permit him to take Haimanti to her father's house. But his father's roar of objection throws cold water on his last-ditch attempt at retrieval. Once bursting into a short-lived flame of energy, he lapses into patented torpor. He is a wiseacre and a nincompoop who knows he is guilty of pusillanimity but lacks the guts to raise hell.

His self-reproach is instructive: 'Some of my friends have asked me why I refrained from executing what I proposed. What if I forcibly took away my wife? Why did I not do that? Why? If I do not subject the law of truth to the law of popular culture, if I do not sacrifice the dearest person of the household at the altar of the household rules, then why do my veins carry the teaching of the ages? Do you know, the day when the people of Ayodhya demanded the sacrifice of Sita, I too was one among the multitude? And I am one of those ballad-singers who have sung the glory of that sacrifice through the ages. Again, it was I who the other day, wrote an article in a monthly journal narrating the virtues of forsaking the wife for the sake of people's appeasement. Who knew that I would have to write the story of the second sacrifice of Sita with the blood of my heart?'

The restrictive joint-family mores which enjoin almost unquestioned allegiance to parental decree stand in his case in the way of independent action.

The husband of the deaf-and-dumb Subha (*Subha*) who forsakes her for her physical debility is not weak-minded but cruel and heartless, but his second marriage definitely leaves the hapless mute girl in an unmitigable state of life-long suffering.

The young would-be groom of *Aparichita* (The unknown woman) is another specimen of the unassertive compromiser type who does not raise his voice of protest when his maternal uncle weighs his would-be bride's ornaments and departs, disspirited and helpless, to lead the life of celibacy with memories of the unknown woman resonating deep down in his unsatiated soul.

It is however the indifferent husbands whose careless non-interest and lack of rapport with their wives spell doom for them.

The indifference of Gopinath to the burgeoning youth of his wife (Giribala) in *Manbhanjan* (Breaking the ice) ['Somehow Giribala's transition from girlhood to full-grown youth has escaped the notice of her husband.'] has resulted in her emancipation into the free world of the theatre when, in order to take revenge on his uncaring husband she joins the same theatrical group which is the centre of Gopinath's attraction.

Giribala's emancipation is the first step towards Tagore's experimentation with a chain of liberated women—Mrinal (in *Streer Patra*/The wife's letter), Anila (in *Poila Nambar*/The No. one), Bostomi (in *Bostomi*/The Baishnava woman).

No anodyne solution this for distanced/estranged wives in the hallowed household contours, for in those days theatres were not much respectable centres for women's refuge/ occupation. But Tagore conceives of this solution on the pay-you-back-in-your-own-coin formula, for Gopinath's chief intoxication lies with theatrical performances (at Gandharva Theatre).

In *Nashtanir* (The broken home) the entry of Amal into the heart of love-starved Charu takes place through the fissures of relationship between her and her editor husband Bhupati inevitably created by the indifference of the latter to the gradual unfolding of his wife's youth:

> 'In this way by the time he was engrossed in his newspaper obligations, his girl bride Charulata slowly stepped into youth. This great news item remained outside the ken of the newspaper editor's knowledge.'

And therefore 'the first flush of the light of love which makes the husband and the wife appear for ever new to each other bypassed them, and neither came to know when the golden-beamed morn of conjugality dawned in the unconscious state of their life. Without getting the taste of novelty each remained old, familiar, habitual to the other.'

The resultant distancing between the husband and the wife cannot be bridged even after the departure of Amal, such is the gravity of the rupture between them.

The above extracts from the story are enough to show the strong negation of the bio-emotive urge on the part of the husband which is very crucial for a burgeoning conjugality. This is also the root cause of Giribala's husband-revulsion and Anila's (*Poila Nambar*/The No. one) leap into the uncharted and unknown future away from the secure confines of home. In the last-named story it is her husband Adwaitacharan's continued indifference to her psycho-physical needs that leads to the tragedy of husband-wife rupture. The final offer of assistance, which is Platonic in essence, by Sitangsumouli is spurned because the prospect is hardly recuperative of the waste of a whole span of conjugal bliss. Similarly the final ill-orchestrated re-union between Bhupati and Charu cannot ensure unalloyed happiness.

They are indifferent husbands—this Bhupati, Adwaitacharan, Gopinath—repenting after the sad realization of the loss of a precious chapter in life. However there are men who love their wives, but it is vegetative love and that too is ruptured beyond repair for a crucial lapse on their part. Such is the predicament of Chhidam (in *Shasti/* Punishment) who names his innocent wife Chandara as the killer of his sister-in-law in order to save his elder brother from the gallows. Out of a tremendous shock and vehement umbrage over the unexplained perjury on her husband's part Chandara refuses to utter the tutored language of defence to save her life, falsely confesses to her crime and goes to the gallows to do penance for her brother-in-law's sin and husband's warped sense of priority.

The predicament of Nibaran, the husband of Harasundari (*Madhyabartini*/The in-between girl) is less traumatic but more absurd. He is the not-really-unsatisfied partner of a charmless conjugal relationship, agrees under his wife's persistence to take a second wife and finds charm and novelty in his new lease of married life. But with the death of Sailabala—the second wife—he has a hesitant home-coming which leaves disharmony and absurdity in its trail:

Once at dead of night when the whole city was asleep, Nibaran took slow steps to the lonely bedroom of Harasundari. Silently according to the old customary habit he laid his body on the right-hand side of the old bed. But this time he entered his old rightful kingdom like a thief.

Harasundari did not utter a word, nor did Nibaran. They lay on the bed side by side as on previous nights; but just in the middle lay a dead girl, whom none could cross.

Tragedy however is averted in the life of the blind Kumudini (*Dristidan*/Restoring the eyesight) whose husband returns to the security and confidence of his wife's love after a temporary aberration (his weakness for Hemangini and resolve to marry her are only a passing phase but a dangerous one with ruinous possibilities).

If the love of Nibaran, Chhidam and men of their ilk for their wives is customary and leads to unhappy and sometimes ruinous consequences, that of lovers is not all sunshine either. The sensuality of Mohitmohan (*Bicharak*/The Judge) drags

Hemshashi to the hell of prostitution by deceit and a fake profession of love.

The sensual attraction of a Guru for the body of Bostomi (*Bostomi*/The Vaishnav woman) forces her to leave husband and home, but not as another victim of adultery, but to cleanse her corrupt mind and seek spiritual elevation.

The configuration of sensual lovers is broken by instances of idealism and steadfastness in men in stories like *Rabibar* (Sunday) in which the protagonist Abhikkumar writes to his financée Biva from England promising to come back to her with an attitude of surrender:

> 'As I come far away from you, the unthinkability of love looms with all the brightness in my mind; it has enabled me to cross the thorny barrier of reason and arguments—I can visualize you with a supra-terrestrial grace. So far I sought to understand (you) with my reason, now I want to have (you) with the whole of my heart.'

The steadfastness of Rajib's love (*Mahamaya*/Mahamaya) for the widowed Mahamaya who has returned to life and him from the funeral pyre of her dead husband is proved when he takes her to the safety of a distant place, not as a married wife, but to live together. The resumed love relation is however cut short as Mahamaya sets out of his home into the unknown and uncertain future when Rajiv pries into her burnt face behind her careful but once-removed veil.

There are a host of other male characters in Tagore's short stories that are as varied and heterogeneous as the stories in which they appear. He shows how a revivalist father's (Bhabanicharan in *Rasmanir Chhele*/Rasmani's son) over-anxiety for recovering the lost ancestral glory leads to the premature death of his son, how Anathbandhu's irresponsible and selfish life-style (*Prayaschitta*/Penance) brings untold misery and suffering to the life of his self-effacing wife Bindhyabasini, how a megalomaniac Yagnanath (*Sampatti-samarpan*/Bestowing of property) buries his own grandchild mistakenly for guarding his property as a *Yak* for the benefit of his lost grandchild who is expected to return, how a noble-souled Muslim (*Musalmanir Galpa*/The story of a Muslim woman) saves the life and honour of a newly-married Hindu girl and gives her love and self-respect for her final metamorphosis into a supra-communal identity.

In this way the show goes on until we get a whole spectrum of men who are real and vibrant, contemporary and eternal.

10

SOCIAL CONSCIOUSNESS IN RABINDRANATH'S SHORT STORIES

Gone am I to the skirts of that
    neighbourhood at times;
But I lacked the strength to cross the border.
    Where life mingles not with life,
False theme spoils the musical fare.
    So I accept the calumnious plaint—
The imperfection of my music.
    My poetry, so know I, has gone
Diverse ways, but not everywhere.

(*Aikatan*/Harmony, translated by the author)

Written on January 21, 1941, when, standing on the edge of his long journey through life, the poet was listening to the distant footfall of death, *Aikatan* (Harmony) is the epitome of confessional poetry. He was already criticised for the high-brow slant of his writings, and in this poem he confesses to his alleged lack of rapport with the masses, being relegated to the narrow window-side position of honour in the high stratum of society. The allegation regarding the absence, in his writings, of the picture of those living in the lowest stratum of social hierarchy cannot be totally gainsaid. Yet it is equally true that when he sets about portraying a slice of this life, he is excellent and true to the minute detail, as in the short story entitled *Shasti* (Punishment). He came in contact with the people of all shades including those in the lowest rung of society during his Silaidaha stay and his vision can hardly be flawed in terms of minutiae.

What however hurt him most was the allegation in respect of the portrayal of middle-class life and society. In the essay called *Sahityabichar* (Appreciating Literature) in *Sahityer Swarup* (What is Literature) he writes: "Now it is time I give a reply to those who complain that they fail to find any trace of middle-classism in my writings.... Once, month after month, I wrote stories on village life. I believe, before that pictures of village life were not published in a systematic form in Bengali literature. At that time there was no dearth of middleclass writers, but almost all of them were engrossed in contemplation of Pratap Singh or Pratapaditya. I am afraid, one day *Galpaguccha* would be found untouchable as bad literature for its association with a 'bourgeois writer.'" Rabindranath's prediction has been found to be untrue, for even more than half a century after his death, his short stories have not lost their appeal, whatever critics had to say about them.

The fact is that middleclass life comes alive through the pages of *Galpaguccha* and his perception of this life at the same time reveals a social consciousness which, instead of cutting out any reformist image for him, is concerned with the umpteen ills that plagued that society. He saw how the stranglehold of the Juggernaut of customs and prejudices sapped the being of that society and how men and women sometimes meekly submitted to the will of the Juggernaut. His object is to point out the defects and rouse people's conscience.

In the short stories of *Galpaguccha* Rabindranath has portrayed social problems and their impact on the life of the individual, the interaction of the individual and the family, the fight of the individual to free himself from the numerous ill-begotten yet expendable customs impeding the flow of normal life, the process of marginalization of women in family life in particular and society in general and many such problems afflicting the life of the individual and society.

A look at some of the stories of *Galpaguccha* will be a rewarding exercise in establishing Rabindranath's realist credentials, as opposed to the essentially romantic bent of his mind.

Initial Stage—*Hitabadi* Phase

Rabindranath's flair for writing short stories found an easy outlet in a number of journals—*Hitabadi*, *Sadhana*,

Bharati, Prabasi, Sabujpatra etc. some of which he himself edited. It was in *Hitabadi* that he started writing short stories. In his own words, 'The journal called *Hitabadi* was born before *Sadhana*.... In that journal I wrote a short story every week, reviews and literary essays. My short story writing began in that journal. I wrote for six weeks' (letter written to Padmini Mohan Neogi).

His mind was already exercised over one of the major evils of the society—the question of dowry and its tragic consequences—the torture and tribulation inflicted on the daughters of indigent and insolvent fathers in their in-laws' houses often resulting in their death. He wrote in *Prabasi* of Ashadh, 1348 B.S.: 'I have seen...the unredeemed animosity of the mother against the daughter-in-law....' The picture of the in-laws' house with all the control vested in the redoubtable father-in-law and the sharp-tongued mother-in-law operating the machine of torture left a deep impression on his mind. *Sasurbari* is synonymous with prison. Hence in the very insipient stage of his writing short stories he draws a lurid picture of torture and death in the in-laws' house of a girl whose indigent father fails to provide sufficient dowry for her daughter. *Denapaona* (Dowry) is a saga not of Nirupama's woes alone, but of the thousands of such hapless girls whose fathers fail to meet the rapacious demands of their in-laws at the time of, and after their marriage. The following extract from the story is indicative of the suffering inflicted upon such hapless girls through the centuries:

> "Nobody cares even for the basic necessities of the daughter-in-law, like food and clothing. If any kind-hearted neighbour mentions some lapse, the mother says, 'That is quite enough.' In other words, if her father paid in full, the daughter would have received cent per cent care. Everybody behaves in a way as if the daughter-in-law has no right here, as if she has entered the household through fraud" (Translated).

But Nirupama's sense of self-respect roused when her father brings money by selling his homestead is symbolic of the resistance against such oppression on the part of the oppressed themselves. No doubt she dies, but not before raising her voice of protest:

> "Niru said, 'If you make any payment of money, it amounts to insult (of mine). Do you think your daughter has no dignity? Am I a money-purse only, that as long as there is money, I have value! No, father, please don't insult me by giving them the money. Moreover, my husband doesn't want it.'"

Society encouraged and indulged in this rape of helplessness, for after the death of Nirupama, the mother writes to her son about his impending second marriage which will fetch a dowry of twenty thousand rupees and that too in cash!

The other story of this phase, having a social flavour is *Ramkanaiyer Nirbuddhita* (Ramkanai's folly) which brings out another kind of greed—misappropriation of property. Ramkanai, the old simpleton, frustrates the nefarious design of his son and wife to deprive his sister-in-law of her husband's property bequeathed to her by a makeshift will written by Ramkanai himself and illegibly signed by his dying elder brother. In the law-suit that follows Ramkanai stands for truth resulting in the imprisonment of his dishonest son for forging his uncle's will. Ramkanai's unlamented death at the end of the story brings into sharp focus the difference between the dwindling breed of honest 'simpletons' and the thriving breed of dishonest do-nothing but 'clever' people in society.

Ugly Offshoots

The dowry system with its ugly offshoots handed down from a feudalistic past so deeply convulsed Rabindranath's mind that in a story called *Aparichita* (The unknown woman) he unravels the nakedness of a feudalistic mindset which does not baulk at robbing the sacramental bond of marriage of all its decency and dignity. The picture of the bridegroom's maternal uncle weighing and testing the purity of the bride's ornaments points to an ugly relic of the feudalistic marriage system in which the bride is looked upon as nothing more than a money-fetching instrument. The break-down of so many marriages at the ceremony itself because of non-fulfilment of dowry commitments is not rare even today. But side by side with this picture of ugliness Rabindranath presents another picture—that of self-dignity, first on the part of the bride's father, Sambhunath Sen who refuses to give his daughter in marriage to a member of such a mean-minded family, saying, 'I cannot give my daughter in marriage to a family the members of which think that I have stolen my daughter's ornaments,' and secondly, on the part of the bride, Kalyani, who remains a lifelong spinster by way of protest against such an ugly insult.

Even in *Yagneswarer Yagna* (Yagneswar's ceremony) the profligate spree of wasting *chhana* of Yagneswar by the members of the bridegroom's party who consider their right to do anything they like as inviolable is described with a trenchant realism. But the story does not end on this ugly note, for soon the groom comes forward to protest and distribute the *chhana* himself. The voice of conscience does not always remain smothered.

Another member of this up-and-coming rebel group that goes against the rigid norms of feudalistic fathers is Hemanta—the protagonist of the story named *Tyag* ('Forsaking')—who refuses to submit to the parental *fatwa* of abandoning his wife Kusum because of her lower caste. Hemanta places love above caste and says on the face of his rigid father, 'I will not leave my wife.' Rabindranath's abhorrence of caste-prejudice is no less pronounced.

Haimanti (the tortured daughter-in-law of the story bearing her name) is not however as fortunate as Kusum. Her husband is at the opposite end of the spectrum—a spineless and weak-kneed type of young man who knows no resistance to the parent's will. So Haimanti compensates for her father's lack of wealth by her own life.

New Turn

Rabindranath's socio-familial concept took a new turn as he began to probe the husband-wife relationship within the joint family set-up. Gone is the tyrannical in-law and submissive son syndrome in which subservience to the patriarchal norm is *de riguer*, as Rabindranath seriously sets out, at the beginning of the present century, to apply his mind to the taboo subject of women's emancipation.

Nashtanir (The broken home) serialised from Baishakh, 1308 B.S. in *Bharati*, breaks a new ground, for it explores the depth of the socially unsanctioned love—love at the extra-marital level. The extra-marital love between Amal, Bhupati's cousin who pursues his higher studies at the latter's house and Charulata his young wife who graduates from girlhood to full-blown youth behind his knowledge because Bhupati remains terribly preoccupied with his editorial duties for his self-owned English journal, is not within the parameters of the prevailing social mores. Rabindranath does not make Charu another persecuted Haimanti, but probes human relationships within the context of the joint family set-up. Amal becomes Charu's surrogate companion who fills Bhupati's place in the emotional life of a burgeoning young girl and the loving relationship that develops between Charu and Amal ruins Bhupati's home. The husband's stolid neglect gives Charu the chance to find emancipation in extra-marital love. Charu is the precursor of Mrinal (*Streer Patra*/The Wife's Letter) and women of her ilk who are products of Rabindranath's rationalistic thinking, that unfolds itself in his *Sabujpatra* phase, on the woman's position in the socio-familial life.

In this phase—in which Rabindranath accords an apotheosizing welcome to Youth in the *Balaka* sequence of poems—he veers away from the traditional socio-familial image of the Indian woman—the mother image, the daughter image, the suffering daughter-in-law image—and sets a new value-judgement for the woman. The aging poet's welcome to Youth has its corollary in the concept of the rebel woman who does not accept her husband's neglect lying down, but revolts, not in a violent, but silent manner. The poet's foreign travel and exposure to the socio-familial life-pattern of the West and the idea formed about the emancipated woman moulded this progressive outlook of his. The Indian woman, at the beginning of the present century, knows no divorce, nor does the revolt end up in the kind of drastic step that Mrinal takes. But Rabindranath's women in a number of stories written in the *Sabujpatra* phase—Mrinal (*Streer Patra*), Kalyani (*Aparichita*), Anila (*Poila Nambar*)—show an individuality as yet unheard of in contemporary Bengali literature and even life itself. Rabindranath, the seer, anticipates the shape of things to come and in this case, his is not an example of Art Imitating Life, but the other way round.

Streer Patra is a collage of events happening in a joint family that result in gradual disaffection of Mrinal who refuses to be tethered to the blood-sapping chores and suffocating household confines and to submit to the untrammelled sway of prejudices and superstitions in the family. A meaningful conjugal relationship might have mitigated her discontent. The sad death of Bindu, the sister of her elder sister-in-law is the proverbial last straw on the camel's back and she leaves the household and husband for the peace of Srikshetra and the pleasant ambience of the outside world where she can find her true bearing in life. The voice of revolt heard from among the lines of her letter to her husband serves as a bombshell on the prejudice-bound psyche of the patriarchal society:

> 'You kept me blanketed under the darkness of your habits. Bindu came for a short space of time and surveyed me through an aperture of that cover. That girl through her own death tore that cover asunder from end to end. Today on coming outside I know not where to keep my glory.'

This bombshell of non-conformism and the picture of the emancipated woman really drew protests from the conservative and reactionary upholders of socio-familial norms (cf. protests of Bipin Chandra Pal and Lalit Chandra Bandyopadhyay in the monthly journal *Narayan*).

If Kalyani's (*Aparichita*) spinstership and devotion to social work as the mission of her life is a silent but meaningful protest against the ugliness of the dowry system, Anila's (*Poila Nambar*/The Number One) flight from home is a silent but forceful protest against the neglect of her book-worm husband, Adwaitacharan. Haimanti's litany of woes in *Haimanti* does not break the beat of this continuum of a progressive picture of the women of the *Sabujpatra* phase of Rabindranath's writings, for her individuality is no less pronounced in the story.

Other Evils

In some short stories Rabindranath touches, sometimes

sarcastically, upon some other evils of the society born out of blind customs and unhealthy traditions. The sanctimonious concept of the sanctity of the precincts of a Hindu temple is treated, rather satirically, in the story called *Anadhikar Prabesh* (Intrusion) in which Jaikali the sanctity-conscious widowed owner-custodian of Lord Radhanath temple gives shelter to a young pig inside the sanctum of the shrine to save it from a rushing group of *Doms*. The last sentence of the story contains the satirical tone of Rabindranath:

> The Supreme Lord of living beings was much pleased at this insignificant incident, but the small locality's much smaller god called Society, became very much excited.

A short while before his death Rabindranath wrote a story called *Musalmanir Galpa* (The tale of a Muslim woman) in which he twists the warp of the untouchability theme with the woof of the theme of communal prejudice. Kamala, saved by the old saintly Samaritan, Habir Khan from being waylaid by the notorious bandit Madhumollar and his men, while on her way to her in-laws' house in her nuptial dress and finery, accompanied by her newly-married husband and guards, is refused entry into her uncle's household, marries Habir's second son and saves her uncle's daughter from a similar plight, when she is on her way to her in-laws' house. The story is significant because Kamala, in her changed vision of life, echoes Gora's microcosmic view of a casteless society:

> 'The god who has given me shelter is my god—he is neither Hindu, nor Muslim. I worship him for that honour of love' (Translated).

Though overshadowed by the tale in *Prayaschitta* (Penance) of a shameless self-seeker who rides roughshod over his self-effacing innocent wife by playing false with her (Anathbandhu deceives Bindhyabasini by marrying an English woman during his stay in England for study), the custom of doing penance for crossing the *kalapani* is satirised in the story as a secondary theme.

Namanjur Galpa (Unapproved story) and *Sanskar* (Reform) expose the self-delusion and false humanism of the so-called patriots and social workers. In the first story the social worker/patriot Anil's love for Amiya, the college girl turned worker of the non-cooperation movement evaporates when he is apprised of Amiya's birth story and in the second another social worker Kalika refuses to give a lift in her car to a sweeper because of his calling.

In *Durbuddhi* (Foolhardiness) Rabindranath exposes the corruption in the police administration and also the police-medical practitioner unholy nexus.

Rabindranath's perception of life in general and society in particular embraces all shades. In the *Tin Sangi* (Three companions) group of short stories—*Rabibar* (Sunday), *Shesh Katha* (Last tale) and Laboratory—he casts a piercing look at the goings-on of the neo-Anglophiles among the urban elite and finds them hollow. Indeed, Rabindranath is a socially conscious artist whose short stories, *inter alia,* give a wide spectrum of life and society—multicoloured and variegated. The charge of his aversion to realism is only a canard.

INDEBTED TO

1. *Galpaguccha*—Rabindranath Tagore (complete edition).
2. *Rabindra-sahityer Bhumika*—Niharranjan Ray, 1369 B.S.
3. *Rabindranather Chhotagalpa O Upanyas*—Upendranath Bhattacharya, 1395 B.S.

11

SUPERNATURALISM IN RABINDRANATH'S SHORT STORIES

The Coleridgian prescription of natural supernaturalism in order to achieve 'a willing suspension of disbelief' with its strictly inverted logic has an echo in Rabindranath's supernatural stories that he wrote mainly between 1298 B.S. and 1314 B.S. The English Romantic poet's natural supernaturalism depends for its execution on a fusion of the natural and the supernatural on the one hand and the real and the fantastic on the other, so that the weird and the uncanny do not raise uneasy questions in our mind about their probability but temporarily lull and suspend our reasoning power and enable us to enjoy the beauty of the world of imagination that Coleridgian supernatural world basically is.

However, the basic component of this world is the picture of the distant and the far-away which easily lends it a mysterious and eerie charm, while in Rabindranath's world of the supernatural it is the here and the now, that is, the much-too-familiar world which gets precedence. Moreover, Rabindranath weaves a web of fantasy and deliberately and wilfully so and at the end of the story when everything is said and done, smashes the glasshouse into smithereens and confesses like Dushmanta confessing to Vidushak after recounting the story of his love-affair with Sakuntala in Kalidas' *Abhignanasakuntalam* that all is told in jest—*'Parihasabijalpitam sakhe!'*

Two-tier method

In the majority of these short stories of Rabindranath there is a two-tier method of telling: the story is not told direct by the author himself, but reported at second hand except *Mastermasay* which is told straight by the writer.

These stories may at first glance appear as off-beat exercises, for Rabindranath wrote only a handful of them: *Kankal* (The skeleton), *Nisithe* (At night), *Kshudita Pashan* (The Hungry stones), *Mastermasay* (The Tutor), though there are a few others like *Sampattisamarpan* (Bequeathing of Property) and *Guptadhan* (The Hidden Treasure) which have been built on our simple belief in supernatural agencies. *Kankal* too might have been left out of reckoning had it not been for an atmosphere of eeriness that Rabindranath builds to some extent here and there. However we shall confine our discussion to the five stories mentioned above and try to study their character.

The belief in ghosts is on the one hand a product of childlike credulity and on the other a product of religious faiths. The belief in after-life and astral state of the soul are the main strands of many religious systems. In the Hindu mind the conception of *Pretlok* (the region of ghosts) is founded on a hoary tradition. Rabindranath's faith in the feasibility of communication with the other world and his execution of planchettes are well-known. Yet the air of make-believe that he creates in all the supernatural stories except *Mastermasay* shows that they have been prompted by their off-beat character and a change in tack.

The technique that he adopts in all these stories is to bring the supernatural elements into the natural world, to combine and unify the ghostly and the real and to present the supernatural as a projection of the protagonist's psyche.

Similarity

A look at these stories reveals a strange similarity of content and mood and technique adopted.

First, all the stories (except *Mastermasay*) have a two-tier structure, adumbrating a 'stories retold' formula. In *Manihara* the story is told by one school master, in *Nisithe*, the mantle falls on the zemindar Dakshinacharan, in *Kankal* this part is played by the skeleton itself, while in *Kshudita Pashan* it is the cotton duty-collector who tells his own story. It is only in

Mastermasay, that the author himself dons the robe of the story-teller.

Secondly, the supernatural content has its bearing only in the parliament of night, sometimes smeared in pitch dark, sometimes faintly lit by a pale moon (in *Manihara* the backdrop for the appearance of the ghost of Phanibhushan's drowned wife is the faint beam of the ten-day old moon of the dark lunar fortnight, in *Kshudita Pashan* it is the slim shred of the moon during the dark lunar fortnight which makes the atmosphere eerie and in *Nisithe* the trick is done by the broken yellow shred of the moon of the dark lunar fortnight.

Thirdly, what is most significant about the character of the supernatural world created in these stories is that it is touch-and-go and the flicker of the light of the day is enough to cause its disintegration. In *Nisithe,* for example, what appeared to Dakshinacharan at night as the rib-shattering guffaw of laughter spreading itself on the horizon from the eastern part of the Ganges to the distant western shore, proved during the day to be nothing but the cackle of migratory swans. In all the stories the light of the day tolls the death-knell of this world of supernatural phantasmagoria. The macabre journey of the cotton duty-collector in *Kshudita Pashan* in his half-awakened and half-asleep trance into the 250-year old scenario of Shah Mahmoud ll's marble pleasure castle ends with the break of dawn: "Suddenly startled by a horrible shout, I saw myself seated on my canvas-cot, with my body wet with perspiration—the broken moon of the dark lunar fortnight grew pale in the light of dawn like a patient fatigued from sleeplessness and our lunatic Meher Ali was wending his way on the deserted morning paths shouting—'Hence! Avaunt!' in his customary daily rounds." The pure fantasy woven round the skeleton in *Kankal* also disintegrates with the break of dawn: "At this moment the first crow cawed. I asked (the skeleton), 'Are you still here?' No response came. The morning light entered the room."

Lastly, it is the natural supernaturalism of Rabindranath which gives these stories their distinctive character. It may be reminiscent of Coleridge, but Rabindranath has nurtured the supernatural within the contours of the natural and finally unifies the two to make it an artistic conglomerate. *Kankal,* the story element of which is the child of the speaker's 'sleepless hot brain' has a *realistic, earthy* canvas for its unfolding and mounting. The room with a skeleton hung on a wall, where the speaker has to sleep one night, the passage of time denoted by the church-clock, the slow death of the oil lamp after giving out the last flickers for five minutes spelling darkness in its trail, the sleepless bed of the speaker covered by a mosquito curtain—these are the unmistakable components of a much-too-familiar world which go to form the backdrop against which the supernatural agency has been placed. The atmosphere is worked up when the speaker suddenly feels something living going round his mosquito-curtain groping in the dark for something which it cannot find. This mix-up of the natural and the supernatural is sort of an achievement for Rabindranath for he does not take the reader, like Coleridge, to a far-off and distant region, but operates within the familiar world for creating an eerie atmosphere. In *Manihara* the supernatural is set against a broader canvas aligning the home of Phanibhushan with all its usual trappings and appurtenances with a river where the ornament-adorned skeleton of the drowned Manimalika leads Phanibhushan to be drowned during a fatal sleep-walk. In *Nisithe* nature plays a pivotal role because Dakshinacharan's hallucination of his dead first wife's presence near his mosquito-curtain on the boat in which he and his second wife Manorama are staying at that time is the aftermath of a frightening experience out on a sandy bed near the Padma:

> "A long beam of the moon fell in a swoon on the little waveless, sleepy and motionless strip of water surrounded by the desert sand. We two came to that spot and stood together—Manorama thought something and looked up to my face, her shawl fell suddenly off her head. I raised her moonlight-radiated face and kissed her.
>
> At that time in that lonely, desolate desert somebody called out three times, 'Who's she! Who's she! Who's she!'"

In *Kshudita Pashan,* however, Rabindranath takes the reader to a distant uninhabited place called Bareech to reconstruct the images of a bygone age through supernatural fantasies. But this does not detract from his skill in mingling the natural and the supernatural for weaving a supernatural story. *Mastermasay* is another story in which the eerie atmosphere is created out of a faithfully constructed natural situation: Benugopal Majumdar rides with the invisible presence of his dead tutor in a horse-drawn carriage and the horripilation he experiences is not only his alone, but the reader's also.

Psychogenetic shapes

Though sufficiently eerie and mysterious, Rabindranath's supernatural beings are basically psychogenetic shapes, whether grisly like the ornament-adorned skeleton of Phanibhushan's drowned wife, reminding one of the bizzare Life-in-Death in Coleridge's *Rime of the Ancient Mariner* or subtly perceptible like the ghost of Benugopal's tutor, Haralal.

The history of the conjugal relationship between Phanibhushan and Manimalika shows a surreptitious weakening of the bond between them. With her stolid disaffection for her husband Manimalika's only passion was for gold: 'She had no offspring in the family; true, she had her husband, but she did not feel his existence in her heart, so she felt a cold shudder down her spine thinking that what was her only object of care, what was growing gradually from year to year like her son, what was not just a symbol, but real gold and jewel, what was to adorn her breast, her neck and her head—her long-cherished and much sought-after wealth—would be sunk in a trice into the fathomless chasm of business.' So she decided to take her wealth to the safety of her father's house in the absence of her husband and got drowned in the river. Phanibhushan's eager wait for the return of his wife reaches such a crescendo that he becomes obsessed and this obsession is transformed into the sound of his supposedly returning wife's ornament-heavy footsteps. Rabindranath has very skilfully employed the jingle of ghostly ornaments and thumping of ghostly footsteps to create an eerie atmosphere. Phanibhushan's vision of his drowned wife's skeleton, his Lady Macbeth-like sleep-walk and ultimate drowning in the river while pursuing in sleep the retreating skeleton are a series of incidents which have their genesis in his beleaguered mind.

The unseen presence of Dakshinacharan's dead first wife and his auditory illusion of the frightful thrice-repeated two-syllable question 'Who's she!' are inevitable projections of his guilt-oppressed mind for indulging in extra-marital love before the death of his disabled first wife.

The unseen presence of Haralal's ghost in the horse-drawn carriage may be supposed to be a projection of Benugopal's guilty conscience for stealing money from Haralal's custody, but a more satisfactory explanation must also take into account the knowledge of the coachman of the ghostly presence in his coach. Haralal's ghost is thus both subjective and objective and is co-equal to the idea of a psychological phenomenon and the age-old idea of the unsatiated soul craving for peace.

The speaker's hallucination of the skeleton in *Kankal* is a product of his hot brain, while the fantasies of *Kshudhita Pashan* too are the product of the cotton duty-collector's imaginative mind.

Rabindranath's supernatural agencies have a psychological basis and in this sense are different from Coleridge's. The name of Coleridge is relevant because of the reference in *Manihara* to the Romantic poet of the supernatural and the Ancient Mariner. One critic, after alleging its 'derivative' character has shown parallels between *Nisithe* and Edgar Allan Poe's story *Leigia* and has faulted the 'near-pathetic' description of the mysterious guffaw of laughter—Ha Ha—Ha Ha—Ha Ha—passing from the Padma, the sandbar, through all the sleeping villages and towns into the boundless distance gradually becoming fainter and fainter and ultimately reduced to the faintest sound (Pratap Narayan Biswas/*Rabindranather Rahasyagalpa O Anyanya Prabandha,* 1984, 19-23). However, there may be parallels with Poe, even close parallels, but Rabindranath's endeavour to create the supernatural atmosphere is neither 'desperate' nor 'pathetic.' He has created a world of temporary make-believe and hence the story-teller is the wine-addict Dakshinacharan, not Rabindranath himself. If at all, he may be compared with Lamb and Keats in this respect, who make similar odysseys into the world of imagination in their characteristic styles (*cf. Dream-children*:

A Reverie and *Ode to a Nightingale* respectively). Or he may be looked upon as the eternal child who constructs and then breaks, and derives pleasure out of this off-the-track game.

12

Rabindranath and Lalan Fakir

Rabindranath's Baul connexion is an accredited fact, but there are divergences of opinion as to his connexion with the great Baul singer of Siuriya village near the sub-divisional headquarters of Kushtia (now in Bangladesh), named Fakir Lalan Shah who occupied premier position in the domain of Baul songs and culture for more than a hundred years (Lalan was said to have been born in 1774 and died 116 years later in 1890).

Two Views

There are two extreme sets of views as to the influence of Fakir Lalan Shah on Rabindranath. Lalan's disciples (Bholai Shah, for example) thought, and propagated the theory, that the MS. *Khata* containing Lalan's songs that Rabindranath took away from the Fakir's Siuriya *akhra* (monastery) formed the basis of the great poet's English *Gitanjali* that brought him world-wide fame. In other words, they believed that Rabindranath was a disciple of the Fakir and the songs of *Gitanjali* were but a skilled poet's poetical version of their Guru's songs which brought him the Nobel Prize. At the opposite end of the spectrum is the view of litterateurs like Annadasankar Roy who thinks that the impact of Lalan on Rabindranath was negligible, at most cosmetic. Annadasankar Roy says, '...the Baul influence on Rabindranath is very limited. The impact of Lalan is much lesser' (*Lalan O Tnar Gan*, a collection of articles in Bengali by A.S. Roy, 1385 B.S., 50).

That the first view is heretical and unfounded by facts is proved beyond doubt by Upendranath Bhattacharya who recounts the story in his magnum opus, *Banglar Baul O Baul Gan* of how he had the privilege of having a look at the

MS. *Khata* containing Lalan's songs on two occasions, both at Siuriya *akhra*, once in 1925 and again some 11 or 12 years later. Then in 1949, he went to Santiniketan on being informed that the MS. *Khata* containing Lalan's songs had been discovered from among the heaps of Rabindranath's old papers. Curiously enough, the MS. *Khata* turned out to be just a copy of the mistake-infested so-called 'real *Khata*' of Lalan. Obviously, Rabindranath collected this 'real *Khata*' of Lalan and had it copied by an old employee of the Silaidaha estate named Bamacharan Bhattacharya and published some of them in *Prabasi* in 1322 B.S. after necessary corrections. The heresy that Rabindranath took away the 'real *Khata*' is set at rest by the fact that Dr. Bhattacharya saw it at the Siuriya *akhra* at least twice, as said earlier. That the concept of love for God with which Rabindranath's English *Gitanjali* is instinct was formed much earlier is quite obvious.

The second view as held by Annadasankar Roy is also not tenable. Rabindranath's Lalan connexion cannot be altogether wished away. His writings, lectures and even songs point a sure finger to this connexion.

Meeting

The writer of *Lalan O Tnar Gan* strongly contradicts the theory that Rabindranath had a meeting with Lalan ('...the meeting between those two luminaries is unsupportable in the absence of proofs.' *Ibid.*, 53).

About his meeting with Lalan there is no uniformity of views. For in a treatise on Rabindranath's songs, Priyabrata Choudhury says, 'There was a talented and very high-class sage poet named Lalan Fakir of Kushtia among the Bauls Rabindranath came in contact with' (*Rabindrasangit*, 1377 B.S., 219). He also quotes Prof. Md. Mansuruddin who says, 'I have learnt from Mrs. Satyendranath Tagore that during their Silaidaha stay Lalan often came to them in their boat. She has referred to Lalan's long back hair. He sang to them quite often. The great world-poet Rabindranath is said to have met Lalan' (*Ibid.*, 220). The poet himself refers to the meetings and discussions between him and the local Bauls when he was at Silaidah (*Ibid.*, 218), but does not mention whether he met Lalan or not. It is not possible that Rabindranath, notwithstanding his position as the young zemindar of Upper Bengal, collected Lalan's MS. *Khata* from his *akhra* without his consent and behind his knowledge. This gives the theory of Lalan-Rabindranath meeting the benefit of doubt. A significant later development is that the Baul character conceived of in his *Falguni* drama was blind, possibly after the one-eyed figure of the great Baul of Kushtia. This conception cannot be based on rumour or hearsay.

Rabindranath's Baul connexion dates back to a quite younger age of his, about 22 or 23, when he had an occasion in Calcutta to listen to a Silaidaha-based Baul who sang to the accompaniment of *ektara* the famous song—

> *'Kothay pabo tare*
> *Amar maner manush ye re!*
> *Haraye sei manushe tar uddese*
> *Des-bidese berai ghure.....'*
>
> (Where shall I find him
> Who is my heart's man!
> Losing him I go about
> In search of him from land to land...
>
> —*Tr. by the author*)

The composer of this song was Gagan Harkara, the postman of Silaidaha and he himself might have been the singer too, though Rabindranath does not mention his name. Whoever be the singer, this is a signpost in the development of his love for Baul songs, for this illiterate singer opened his eyes to the intrinsic merit of the songs of the village Bauls, in which he found echoes of the great Upanishadic concept of *antaratara yadayamatma* (the soul that resides within). The Baul singer's resolve, as expressed in the same song, to find the heart's man within ('*Maner madhye maner manush karo answeshan*') appealed to him most.

The Baul's search for Him is a Guru-guided search, an esoteric pursuit, but when he pines for Him as an Unseen Man ('*aleker manush*'—Lalan), he becomes a mystic and this mysticism of theirs affected Rabindranath also. The eagerness for finding the heart's man, the inner man, the unsophisticated manner of expressing this eagerness, the depth of feeling and above all, the simple and down-to-earth diction of their songs earned the illiterate Bauls of Bengal Rabindranath's love and respect.

Passing Phase

But this realisation of the affinity of the Baul's simple faith with the mysticism of the Upanishadic sage might have been a passing phase in Rabindranath, had he not met a number of Bauls at Silaidaha and heard their songs and therein lies the importance of Fakir Lalan Shah. For Lalan was the kingpin among the Bauls across the Padma, whose songs he heard and who figures in his lectures and writings, though unnamed.

Rabindranath found echoes of the Upanishadic concept of the Unknown Inner Being in Lalan's songs also:

'Achhe yar maner manush apan mane
Se ki ar jape mala!
Nirjane se bose bose dekhchhe khela....'

(Does he who has his heart's man within count the beads!
He witnesses the sport sitting in solitude....

—*Tr. by the author)*

Without naming him, Rabindranath refers in his Oxford lecture to Lalan's affinity with the Upanishadic sage: 'This village poet evidently agrees with our sage of the Upanishad who says that our mind comes back baffled in its attempt to reach the Unknown Being; and yet this poet like the ancient sage does not give up adventure of the Infinite, thus implying that there is a way to its realisation' (quoted by A.S. Roy, *ibid.*, 53). One may refer here to the following song of Lalan in which he hints at how the sought-after Being can be seen:

'Ei manushe sei manush achhe.
Kato munirishi charyug dhare beracche khunje.

....

Amar holo ki bhranti, mon,
Ami baire khunji gharer dhan,
Sirajsain koy, ghurbi, Lalan,
Atmatatva na bujhe.'

(That man resides in this man.

So many sages are searching for him for four millennia.
....
O mind, how mistaken am I,
I seek the inner wealth outside,
Siraj Guru says, Lalan, you will roam about,
Without realising the theory of the self.

—*Tr. by the author)*

Impact

All this resulted in a deep and significant impact of the Baul songs in general and those of Lalan in particular, on Rabindranath. He too thinks of God as *maner manush* (the man of the heart: the inner man) and, like Lalan, becomes self-critical for finding him elsewhere:

'Ami *tarei khunje berai ye roy amar mane mane.*
Se *achhe bole*
Amar *akash jure phote tara rate,*
Prate *phool phute roy bone amar bone...'*
(*Rabindra-rachanabali*, 4th Part, Govt. of W.B., 1368 B.S., 166.)

(I look for him only who resides in my mind.
As he exists
My sky becomes studded with stars at night,
In the morning flowers bloom in forest, my forest.

—*Tr. by the author)*

The 'inner man' concept recurs in other songs of his Puja series:

(i) *'Se ye maner manush, keno tare basiye rakhis nayandware?'*

(He is the man of the heart, why keep him waiting at the doorstep of the eyes?

—*Tr. by the author*)

(ii) *'Amar praner manush achhe prane*
Tai heri tay sakal khane.'

(My heart's man is in my heart,
So I find him everywhere.

—*Tr. by the author*)

(iii) *'Amar mon yakhan jagli nare*
Tor maner manush elo dware.'
(My mind, when you did not wake up,
Your man of the heart came at your doorstep.
— *Tr. by the author)*
(Ibid., 167–68)

These excerpts from Rabindranath's songs clearly show how the *maner manush* concept, first imbibed from Gagan Harkara's song and then reinforced through Lalan's songs, greatly influenced him.

Still it is nobody's case to argue that Rabindranath was completely under the spell of Lalan and/or other Bauls. For in the songs just quoted he combines Upanishadic concept with Lalanic to create a world of his own.

However, the Baul image had its impact in other spheres. Reference has already been made to his creation of the blind Baul character in *Falguni* drama. He himself played two roles in this drama, staged at the Tagores' Jorasanko homestead on 16 January, 1916, of which one was that of Kabisekhar and the other that of the blind Baul. The impact of Lalan's figure is obvious here. As a matter of fact, not only *Falguni,* but other symbolic plays from *Prayaschitta* onwards, have a Baul in their *dramatis personae,* such was the impact of the Baul image on him.

Lalan's influence is also to be noticed in Rabindranath's quoting of two lines in the novel *Gora* from a famous song of the former—'*Khanchar bhitar achin pakhi*' (the unknown bird within the cage). Again the Bhatiali tune of Baul songs appealed to him greatly, so much so that he set this tune to a large number of his songs. Yet any tell-tale influence is difficult to discern in him. He imbibed ideas from many sources, drank deep in many founts, yet, like Shakespeare, transformed everything into his own through the crucible of his imagination and gave what was original ultimately.

It is better to conclude this paper with the words of Rabindranath himself in this regard: 'At Silaidaha I have heard Baul songs from real Bauls and have even seen their old MS. *Khatas.* Without doubt I know that in Baul songs there is a genuine speciality which is modern for all times to come.... Many of my songs are Baul-based, but I have not attempted to copy. They are more obviously compositions of Rabindra-baul' (quoted in *Rabindrasangit* by P. Choudhury, 221).

13

Serious Thoughts in Tagore's Light Playlets

Critics may decry the infiltration of didacticism into the playlets written by Rabindranath between 1292 B.S. and 1294 B.S., and published in *Balak* and *Bharati* journals as *henyalinatya* ('riddle plays') but they are, on the surface, simple sketches. A few of them were meant for the delight of boys, but in real terms, they purvey food for thought for adults, while some others have well-honed appurtenances for satire. Their simplistic garb camouflages an instructive intent also. Truly speaking however, fun is their soul but simple fun-mongering is not their business, for they do not wobble along with pleasant nothings.

These single-theme, humour-oriented playlets looked to the European 'dramatic game' called *charade* for form, as the Preface to the *hasyakautuk* ('humour plays') records: 'These small humour plays were published in *Balak* and *Bharati* under the title of *henyalinatya* ('riddle plays'). These were written to some extent in imitation of a kind of dramatic game known as *charade* in Europe. It was found necessary to shorten the length of these creations in order to keep up the riddle element—hopefully the present readers will not take the unnecessary trouble of tracing that riddle element in them. Some of these 'riddle plays' were especially written for the delight of boys.'

A comprehensive catalogue of these playlets, in which the riddle element lies in the subtle linguistic twists and turns with a sprinkling of pun and innuendo here and there will be useful.

	Name of the playlets	Month of composition	Qualitative identity
(i)	*Chhatrer Pariksha* (The Test of the student)	Sravan, 1292 B.S.	written for the delight of children, but carries adult thoughts
(ii)	*Pete O Pithe* (Food for the Belly and thrashing for the Back)	Ashadh, 1292 B.S.	written for the delight of children and instructive
(iii)	*Abhyarthana* (The Reception)	Bhadra, 1292 B.S.	children's playlet conveying adult thoughts
(iv)	*Roger Chikitsa* (Treatment for the disease)	Jaistha, 1292 B.S.	humorous sketch but instructive
(v)	*Chintashil* (The contemplative one)	Aswin-Kartik, 1292 B.S.	humorous sketch
(vi)	*Bhab O Abhab* (Presence and absence of want)	Agrahayan, 1292 B.S.	humorous sketch
(vii)	*Rogir Baṇdhu* (The Patient's Friend)	Poush, 1292 B.S.	humorous sketch
(viii)	*Khyatir Birambana* (Dangers of Fame)	Magh, 1292 B.S.	satirical sketch
(ix)	*Arya O Anarya* (The Aryan and the non-Aryan)	Chaitra, 1292 B.S.	satirical sketch
(x)	*Ekannabarti* (Belonging to the undivided family)	Baishakh, 1294 B.S.	satirical character-sketch
(xi)	*Sukshma Bichar* (Hair-splitting judgment)	Baishakh, 1293 B.S.	satirical character-sketch
(xii)	*Ashrampira* (Ashramite disease)	Kartik, 1293 B.S.	funny character-sketch
(xiii)	*Antyesti-satkar* (Performance of the Last Rites)	Bhadra, 1293 B.S.	social satire
(xiv)	*Rasik* (The humorous one)	Phalgun, 1293 B.S.	funny sketch
(xv)	*Gurubakya* (The Preceptor's words)	Chaitra, 1293 B.S.	satirical character-sketch

II

Rabindranath's experience as a student of Oriental Seminary was by no means salubrious, but had a far-reaching effect in the evolution of his thoughts on education in his maturer years, which culminated in the setting up of the Ashram School (1901) at Santiniketan. The young sensitive 'Seminary' boy could hardly fit himself into the prevailing mould of education that encouraged negation of the student's individuality and fostered unbridgeable distance between the teacher and the taught. The image of the teacher that was imprinted on his mind in his school days was one of a narrow, impatient, cruel and biased person who hardly thought of earning the student's love, but put the utmost stress on strict adherence to the school syllabi. On the other hand, the system of education introduced by the British rulers of India on the basis of the Macaulayan 'filtration theory' was a hindrance and no help to the development of the student's personality and Rabindranath considered it a 'profound soul-killing folly' (*Sikshar sangikaran*/The assimilation of education). So when he set up the Ashram School, his intention was to revive the education type of the ancient India which laid the greatest stress on teacher-taught proximity and cultivation of a good and healthy relationship between the two. The teacher was a *guru*/preceptor in this scheme of things, whose company enlivened the process of learning and made the growth and development of the student's individuality a highly probable proposition.

A standardisation of this process was Rabindranath's object in giving an ideal system of education to the student community at Santiniketan and this was reflected in all his writings on education also. Thus in his preaching and practice the chief concern was the student and the all-round development of his individuality and personality.

III

The first playlet of his *hasyakautuk* group—*Chhatrer Pariksha*/The Test of the student—shows the travesty of learning as it flounders on a wrong concept of teacher-student relationship. Madhusudan's tutor Kalachand relies on the rod to educate and straighten his wayward student instead of making the learning matter interesting and the result has been the opposite of what is desirable. The relationship between the two turns so sour instead of standing on an even keel that at the guardian's test of his ward in full view of the tutor Madhusudan is actuated by a revenge motive and resolves to call the tutor's bluff:

> 'MADUSUDAN (*Aside*) Yesterday my tutor beat me so hard that my back is still aching. I shall avenge it today and bring about his ouster.'

He resorts to equivocation in answering his guardian's questions, *e.g.*:

> 'GUARDIAN. Well, what is a tree?
> MADHUSUDAN. That which pierces through the earth.
> GUARDIAN. Give an example.
> MADHUSUDAN. Earthworm.'

Again,

> 'GUARDIAN. Well, who finished off Sirajuddaula? What does History say?
>
> MADHUSUDAN. White ants. (*Kalachand canes him.*) Sir, why do you beat me for nothing?—Why Sirajuddaula only, the whole History text book has been finished off by white ants! Look here. (*He shows the book. His tutor scratches his head*).'

In this way the *charade* proceeds through equivocation and innuendos and mischievous tutor-baiting on the part of the student and scolding and caning and embarrassment on the part of the flabbergasted tutor. It is indeed a see-saw battle between the student and the tutor in which the tutor is deliberately upstaged, showing up the stark contours of a jejune system of education which hardly fosters a healthy teacher-student interaction. The playlet ends with both the tutor and the student heaving sighs of relief at a happy riddance from each other.

Abhyarthana (The Reception) shows the ugly underbelly of degree-oriented education which fosters social snobbery, false sense of oneupmanship and uncalled-for swagger. Chaturbhuj Babu's acquisition of the M.A. degree has given him such a false aura of superiority that he tries to make a virtue out of a brazen propaganda of his supposedly extraordinary calibre. The village where he sets his pride-heavy foot all the way from Calcutta does not rise in an open-arm reception to the returning native as anticipated by him, but to his grim chagrin and dismay everybody enquires about his healthy Afghan cat which he carries in tow. Satu Uncle peels the beans when he remarks, 'The young chaps get some education and consider themselves accomplished. No trace of quality—only conceit.' Rabindranath thinks it a pity that instead of arousing modesty, its ideal offshoot, the contemporary education system fosters pride and snobbery—'tail' as Hari uncle suspects:

> 'GIRL. (*Pointing to the backstage*) Come and see Hari Uncle, how fat is the tail!
>
> HARI. Whose?
>
> GIRL. There, his!
>
> HARI. Chaturbhuj's?
>
> GIRL. No, the cat's.'

In *Pete O Pithe* (Food for the Belly and thrashing for the Back) which is a humorous sketch of a bully, Tinkari, the swashbuckler, who snatches a dim-wit child's (Bhutu) *sandesh*, and gives blows on his back, faces an equal torment for his greed when he is treated to hand-made rice-cakes by the child's mother. He gets several blows on his back from Bhutu's grandmother for fun and is also down with indigestion. The instructional content of the sketch is that greed goeth before suffering.

Roger Chikitsa (Treatment for the disease) which is a humour-encapsulated instructive sketch presumably meant for children shows how Haradhan, the goose-thief, is caught and punished by the European physician whose goose he dares steal. His kleptomania however does not get encouragement from his father which is in glaring contrast to the constant encouragement of the maternal aunt of Iswarchandra Vidyasagar's Bhuban who has an equally active habit of stealing and this is the only redeeming factor of this nefarious business, for had Haradhan's father not spoken of taking him to the hospital (Haradhan is taken to hospital by one Mukherjee, though), his kleptomania would have gone undetected and therefore unpunished. The doctor's beating cures him of his stealing habit—

'HARADHAN (*The European Sahib thrashes Haradhan*).

Sahib, no need of (surgery); my disease has been cured completely.'

Chintashil's (The contemplative one) Narahari is a thoughtful type who lapses into deep spells of thought over trifles and makes dithering a way of life:

> 'MOTHER. (*Anxiously*) Child, send me to Benares, I'll live there permanently.
>
> NARAHARI. Well, you may go, mother! Since you wish to live there, I'll not stand in the way.
>
> MOTHER. (*Aside*) My Naru becomes very restless giving his mind to everything. In this matter, however, he did not think long for a decision (*Aloud*). Then you'll have to arrange for some monthly allowance.
>
> NARAHARI. Is't? Then I need to think over it for some time more. It's nothing simple. I'll tell you after a week's thinking.'

He is a faint shadow of Hamlet, exaggerated and caricatured, who spoils everything by pondering.

The majority of the other pieces are spiced with satire, sometimes pungent, sometimes mild, yet driving home the point in a framework of humour and/or fun. In *Rogir Bandhu* (The Patient's Friend), for example, Duhkhiram is the picture of a bad friend for a patient, aggravating rather than alleviating Baidyanath's fear of disease and death. Chintamoni's largely unintelligible pedantic discourses in *Arya O Anarya* (The Aryan and the non-Aryan) is a camouflage for his ignorance and travesty of scholarship. There is a *faux pas* in *Ekannabarti* (Belonging to the Undivided Family) when Daulatchandra's reportedly passionate plea for the continuance of the undivided family system boomerangs on him because the Press reports of his speech delivered at a meeting draw a whole train of distant relatives into his single-member household leaving a nasty pandemonium and complications in its trail. In *Sukshma Bichar* (Hair-splitting Judgment), again, there is a funny sketch of another pedant—Chandicharan—whose delight lies in an animated exercise in irritating linguistic jugglery. This is a satirical sketch of a pedant turned polemical reminiscent of the so-called contemporary scholars who revelled in hair-splitting arguments over trifles. Love of jugglery of words and polemical abstraction is also the stock-in-trade of 'Shiromoni' in *Gurubakya* (The Preceptor's words).

However the sketch of Dukari Dutt, the lawyer in *Khyatir Birambana* (Dangers of Fame) is a humorous study of another side of fame-hungry people who love publicity but at no cost to themselves—material or physical. Mischievous Press reports about his munificence catapults him to overnight fame and he gloats over it, unaware of the mischief done by one Kangalicharan who came to him for a paltry donation to the cause of music and was brusquely dismissed:

> 'It's a real gain! Some Kangalicharan has written in the vernacular Press that I've reportedly donated five thousand rupees to their *Ganonnatibidhayak* club (Music-sponsoring club). No question of donation, I just stopped short of forcibly turning him out. Meanwhile I've become famous—which will be of great help to my business. It'll be helpful to them too; people'll think, since they've got a fat donation, their club is a big one. It'll draw substantial subscriptions from other quarters. However, I'm fortunate.'

The pandemonium that follows with a large train of people of various hues clamouring for donations shows the reverse result of an overweening miserliness. His hasty departure from home for temporary hiding in order to avoid the over-zealous demands of donation-seekers is indeed a lesson for men of his ilk.

An instructive picture of heartless callousness is drawn in the fine satirical playlet—*Antyesti-satkar* (Performance of the Last Rites) which puts up to ridicule the excessive etiquette-mania of four Anglicized Bengalees who complete the nitty-gritty of funeral arrangements before the demise of their Roybahadur father, and print premature obituaries in newspapers. Real grief has no seat—back or front—in their formality-oriented life-style and the eager wait for the moment of death is indicative of the travesty of filial piety, yawning distance between father and children, erosion of values and pompous love for show and prestige:

> 'SKANDA. Those who will join the funeral procession will have to be informed first.

KRISHNA. Son, which is real?—Death or—

CHANDRA. No worry about that, Doctor?

DOCTOR. Yes, Sir?

CHANDRA. How long is father to live? When shall we ask the people to come?

DOCTOR. Perhaps—'

As the Lord of Death has proposed otherwise, Krishnakishore survives amid the din of showy lamentation and the dying man's thin voice announcing his survival pricks. Social satire has never been more pungent.

Index